It's Easy To Play Classic Hits

Classical Music

Film Themes

Jazz, Blues & Soul

Pop & Rock

Classic Hits

Showtunes

Wise Publications
part of The Music Sales Group
London / New York / Paris / Sydney / Copenhagen / Berlin / Madrid / Tokyo

Published by
Wise Publications
14-15 Berners Street, London W1T 3LJ, UK.

Exclusive Distributors:
Music Sales Limited
Distribution Centre, Newmarket Road, Bury St Edmunds, Suffolk IP33 3YB, UK.
Music Sales Pty Limited
120 Rothschild Avenue, Rosebery, NSW 2018, Australia.

Order No. AM993608
ISBN: 978-1-84772-555-4

Edited by Jessica Williams.
Compiled by Nick Crispin.
'Somebody Told Me' and 'Springtime For Hitler' arranged by Derek Jones.
Music processed by Paul Ewers Music Design.
Cover illustration by Liz Barrand.

Printed in the the EU.

Trout Quintet

(4th Movement: Andantino)

Music by Franz Schubert

Canon in D

Music by Johann Pachelbel

poco rit.
Più mosso
mf poco cresc.
f

Für Elise

Music by Ludwig van Beethoven

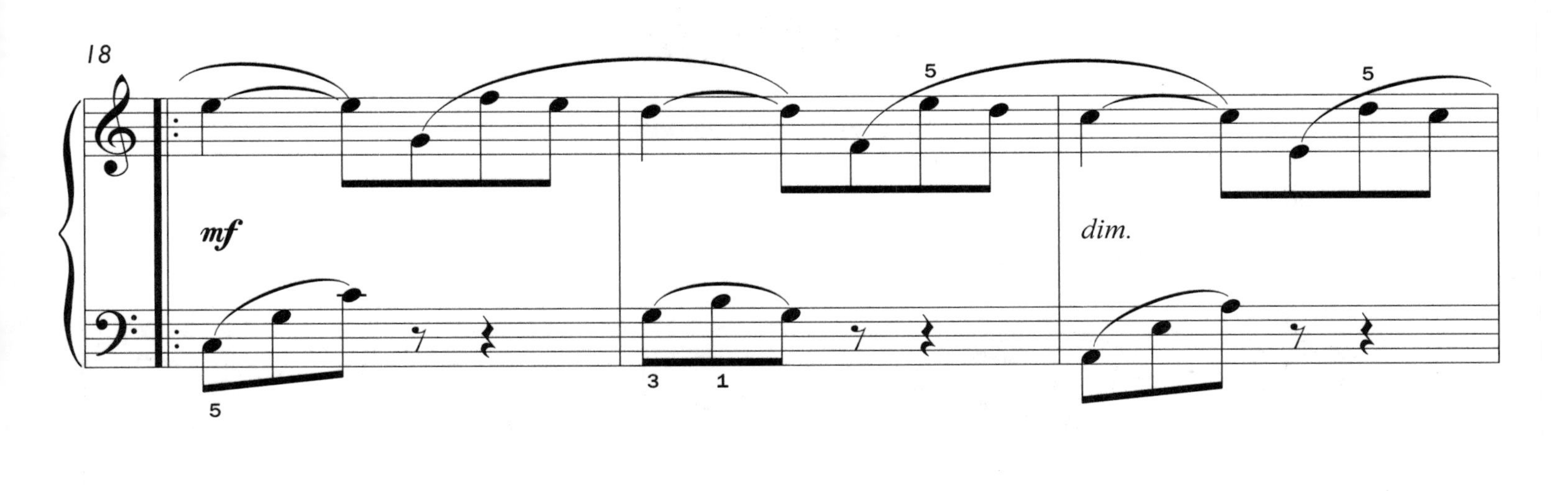
18
mf
dim.

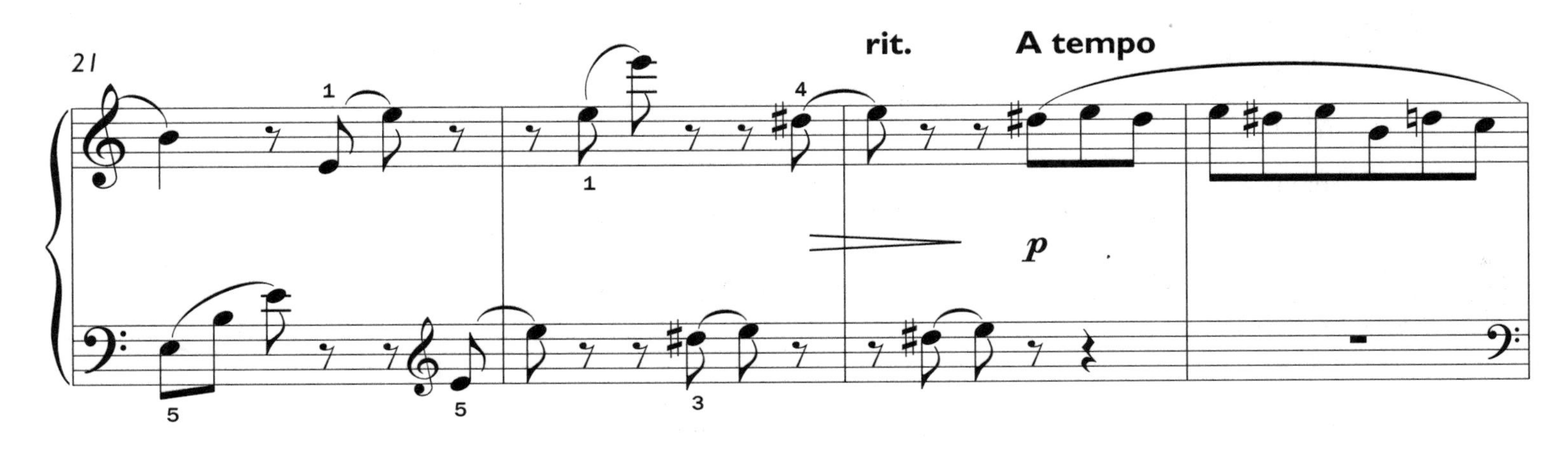
21
rit.
A tempo
p

25

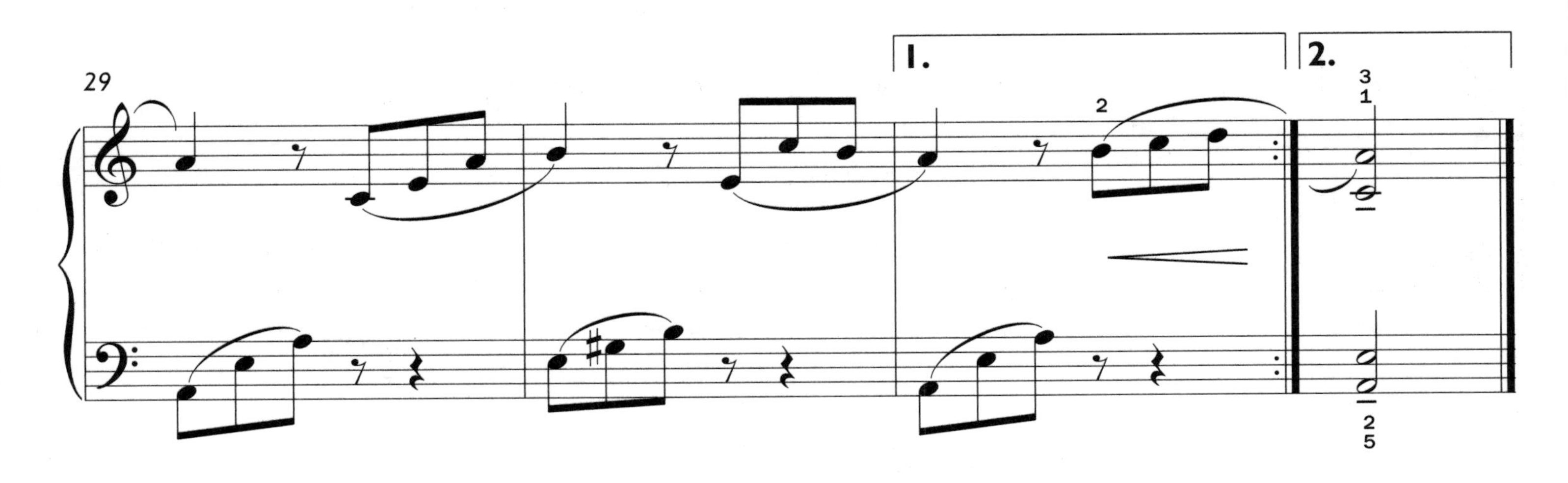
29
1.
2.

Le Onde

Music by Ludovico Einaudi

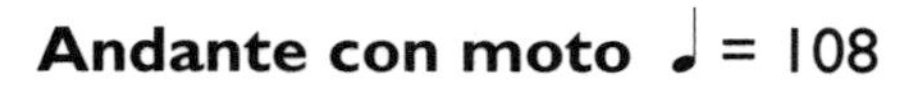

18
mf
dim. poco a poco

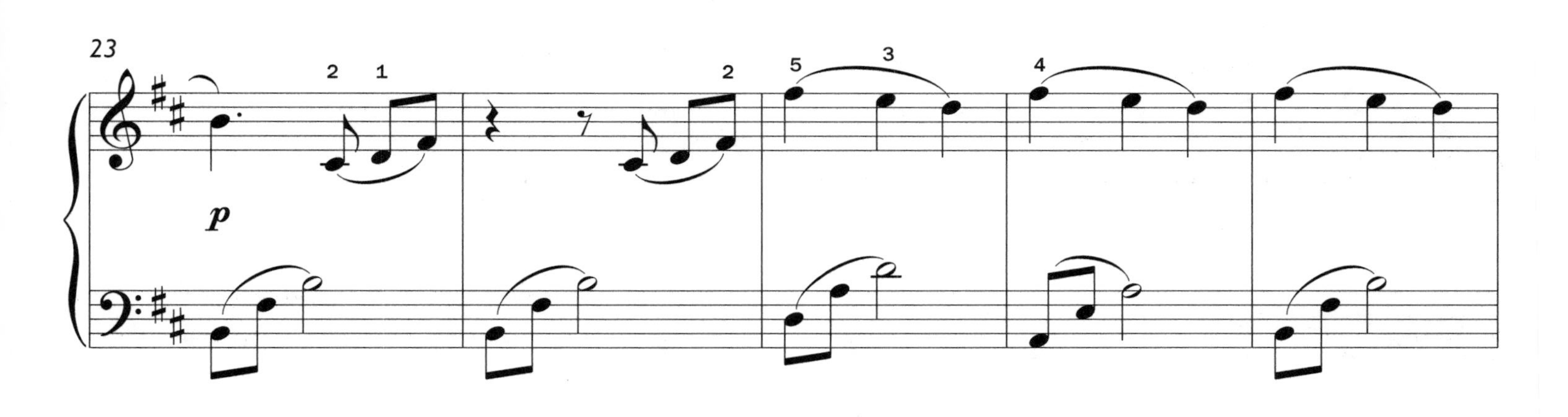
23
p

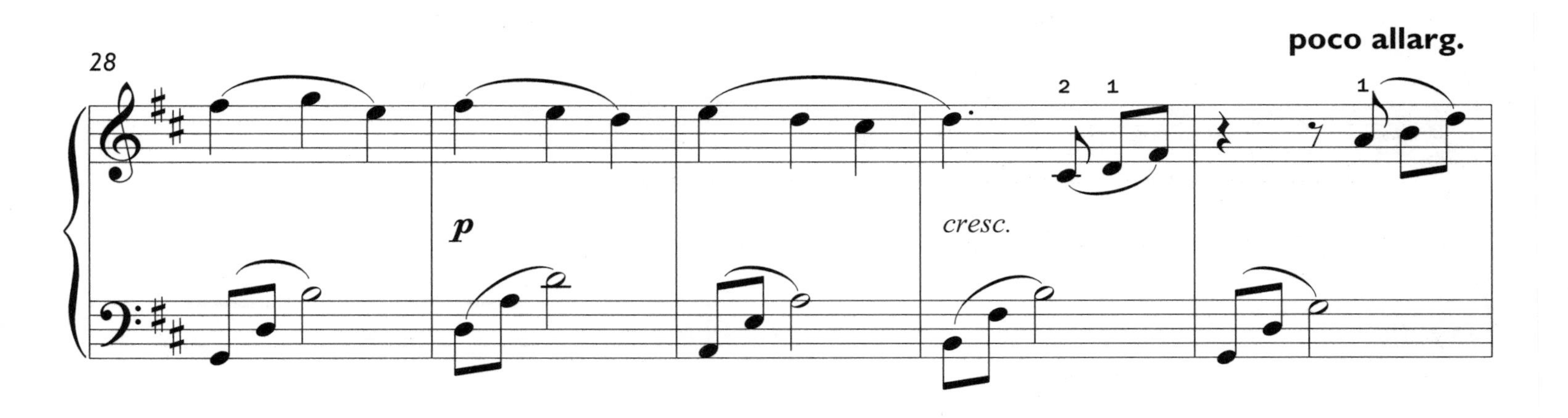
poco allarg.
28
p
cresc.

A tempo
33
mp
cresc.
mf cresc.

allarg.
A tempo
poco rit.
accel.
A tempo

55
mf
dim. poco a poco

59
p
mf

allarg.
A tempo
63
p

67
dim. poco a poco

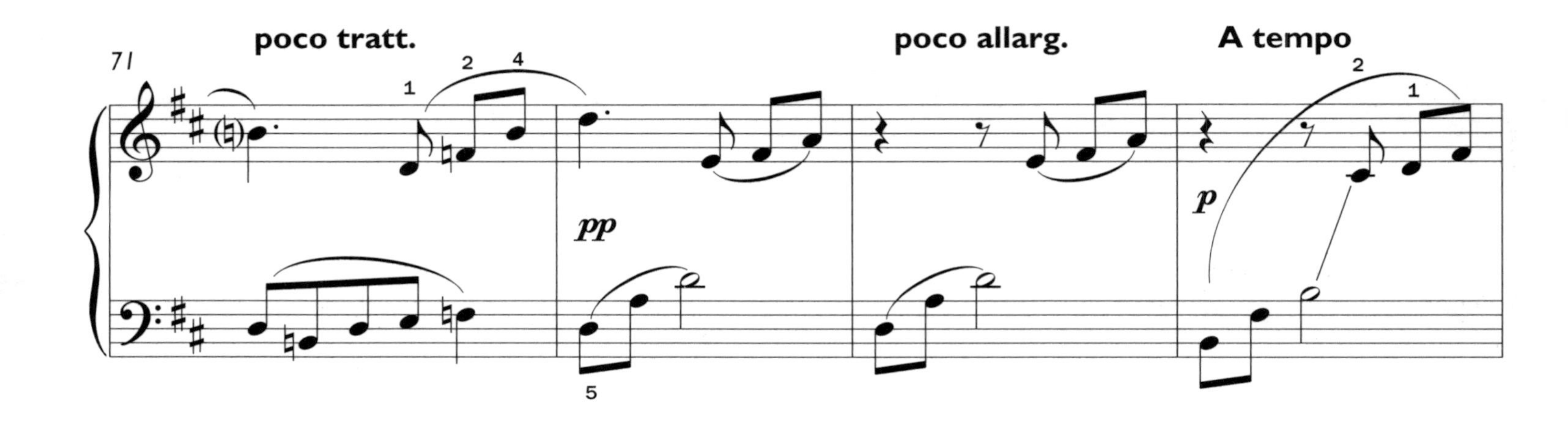
71
poco tratt.
poco allarg.
A tempo
pp
p

75
sim.

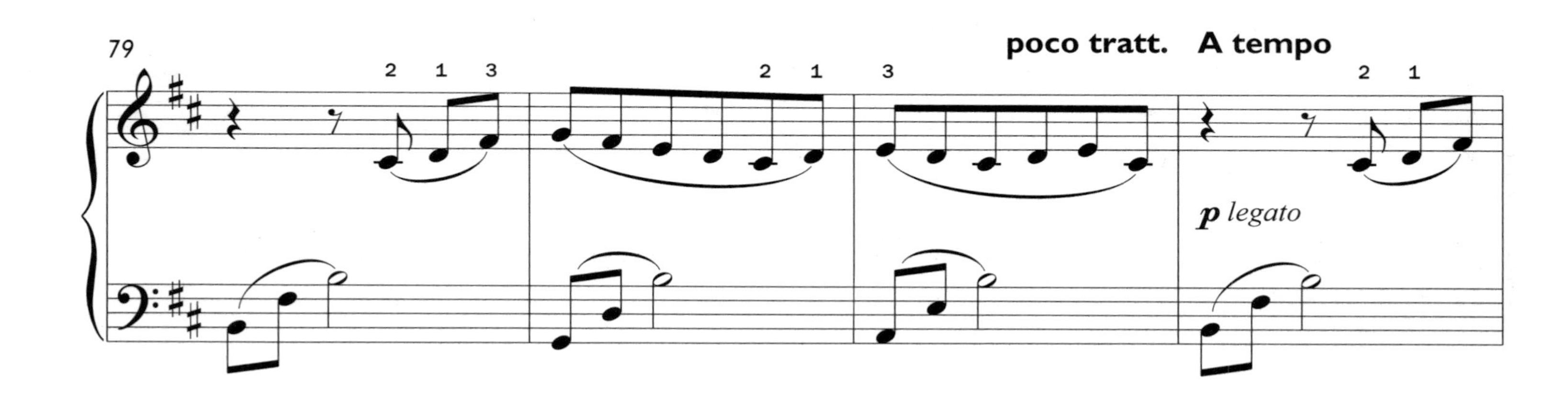
79
poco tratt.
A tempo
p legato

83
pp

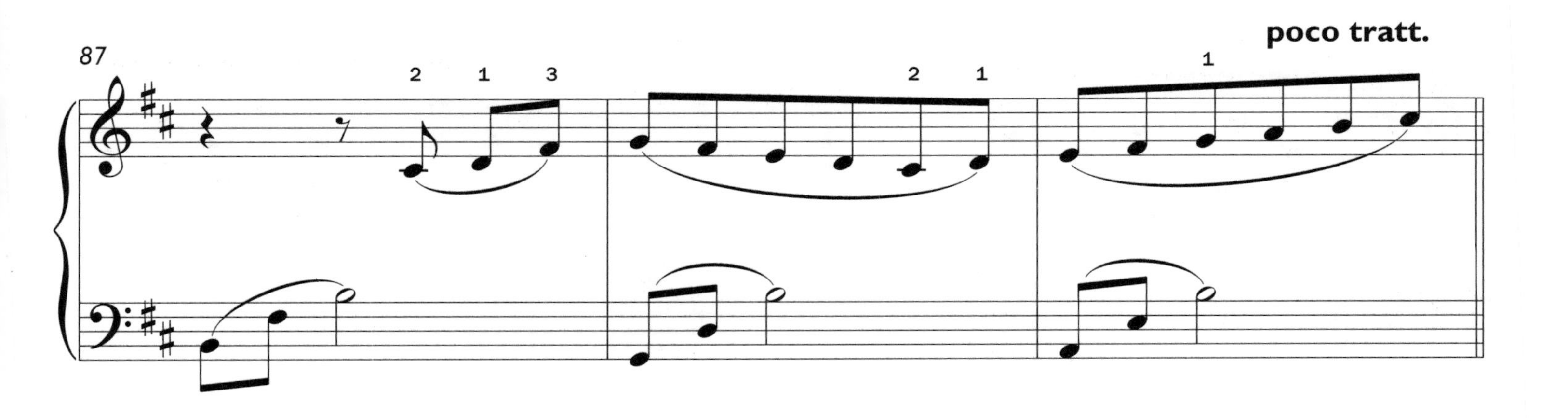
87
poco tratt.
2 1 3
2 1
1

A tempo
allarg.
90
5 1 4 1 3 1
5 1
5 1 2

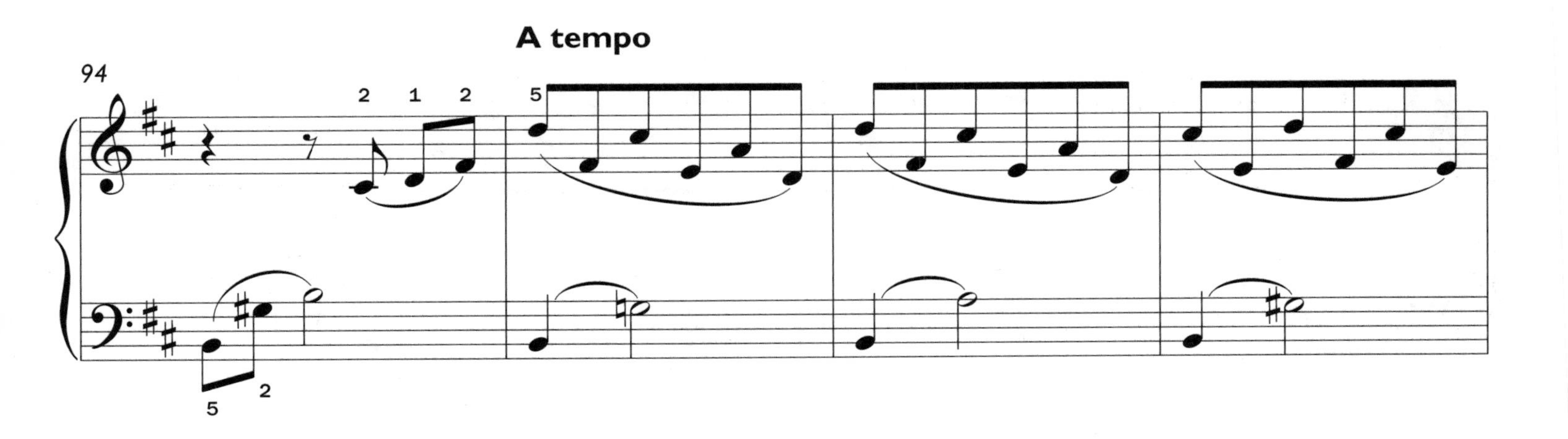
A tempo
94
2 1 2
5
5 2

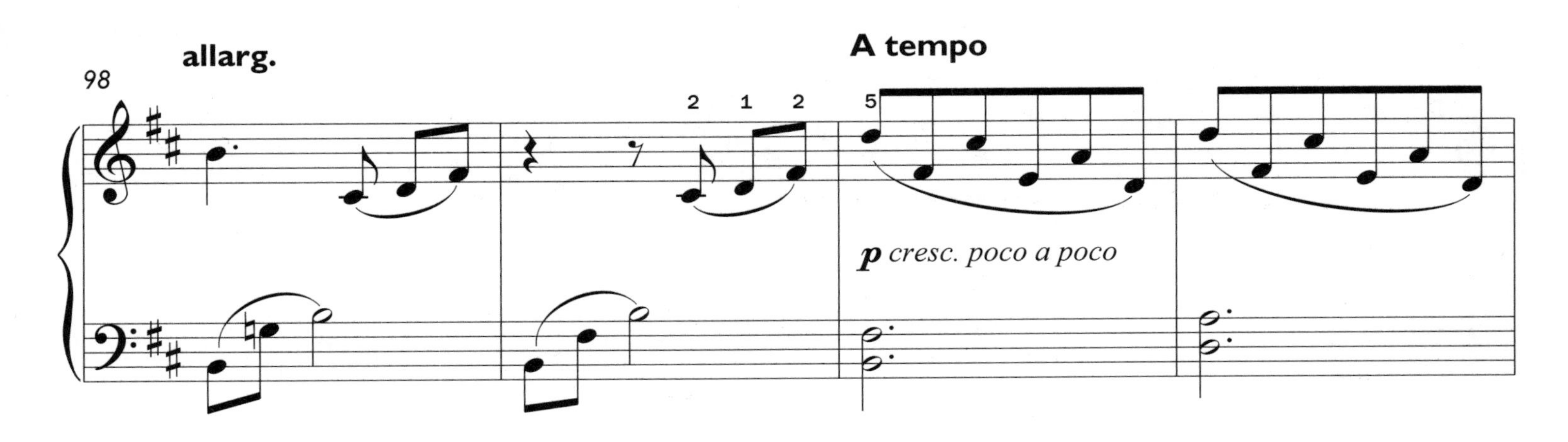
allarg.
A tempo
98
2 1 2
5
p cresc. poco a poco

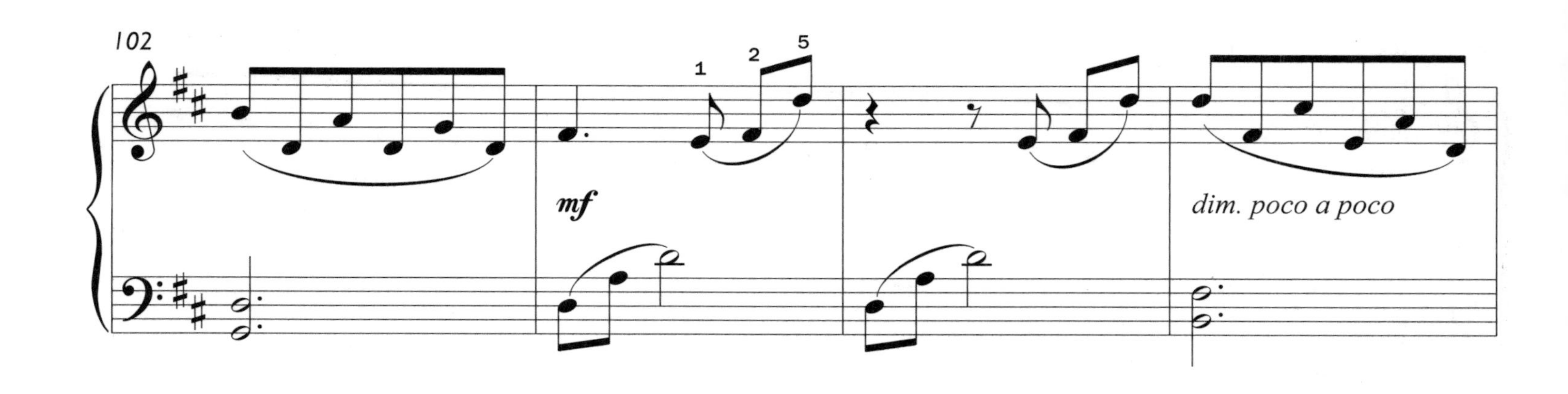
102
1
2
5
mf
dim. poco a poco

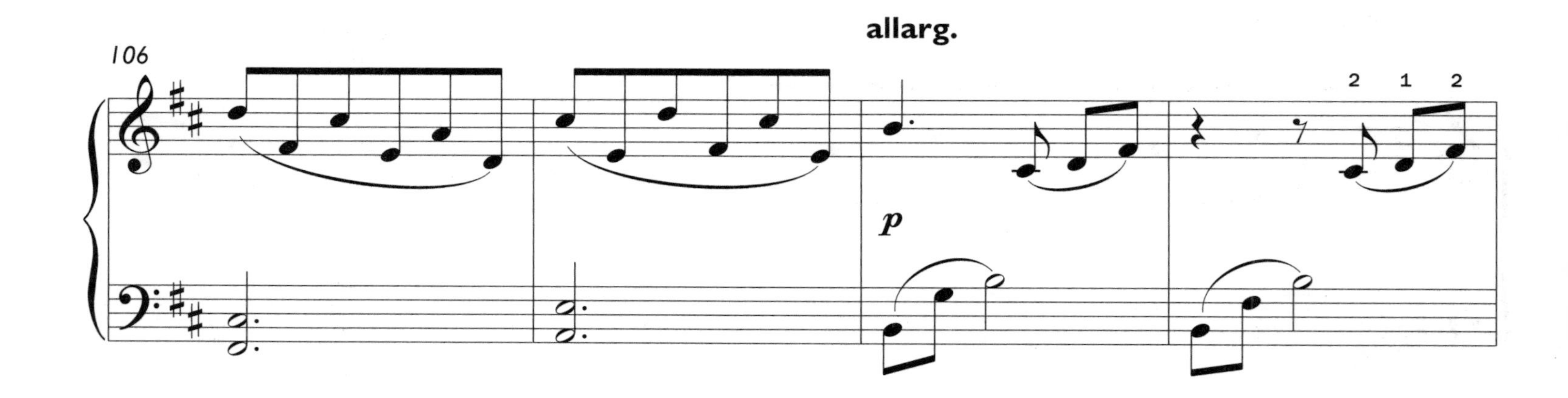
allarg.
106
2
1
2
p

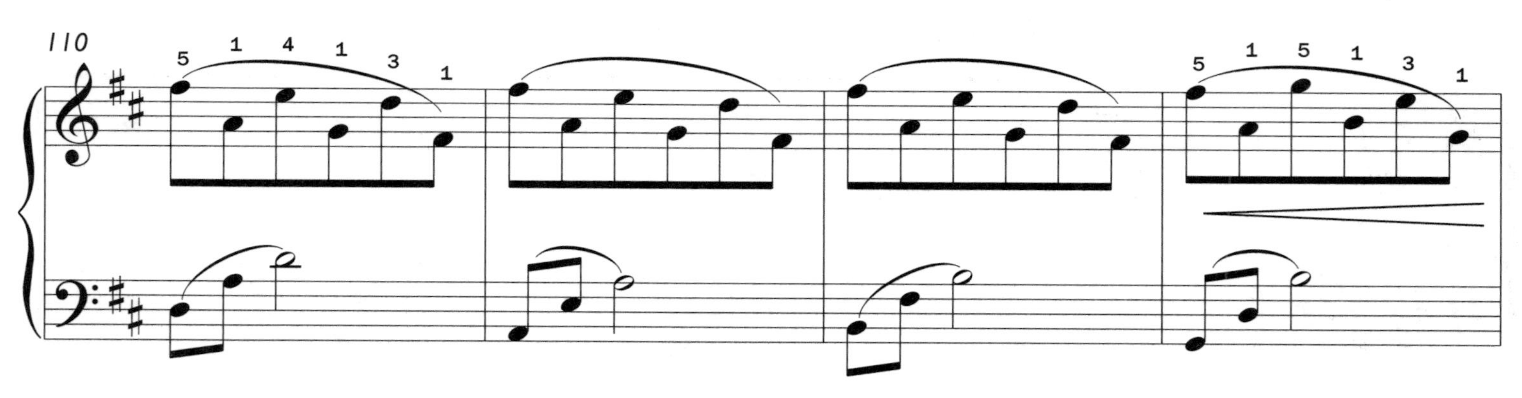
A tempo
110
5
1
4
1
3
1
5
1
5
1
3
1

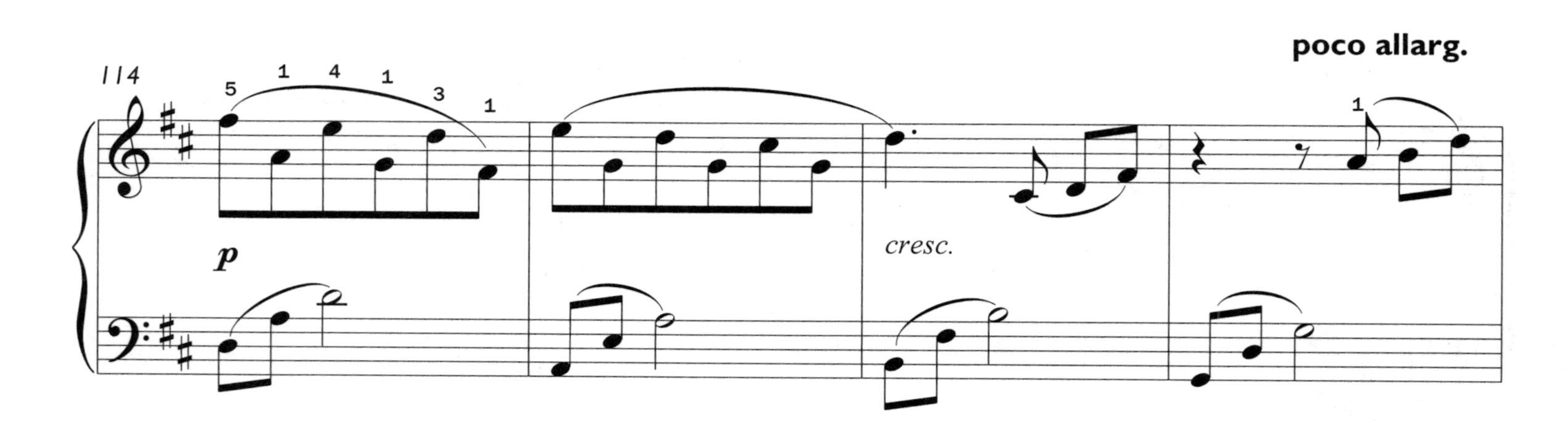
poco allarg.
114
5
1
4
1
3
1
1
p
cresc.

A tempo

118
mp
cresc.

allarg.
122
mf cresc.
f

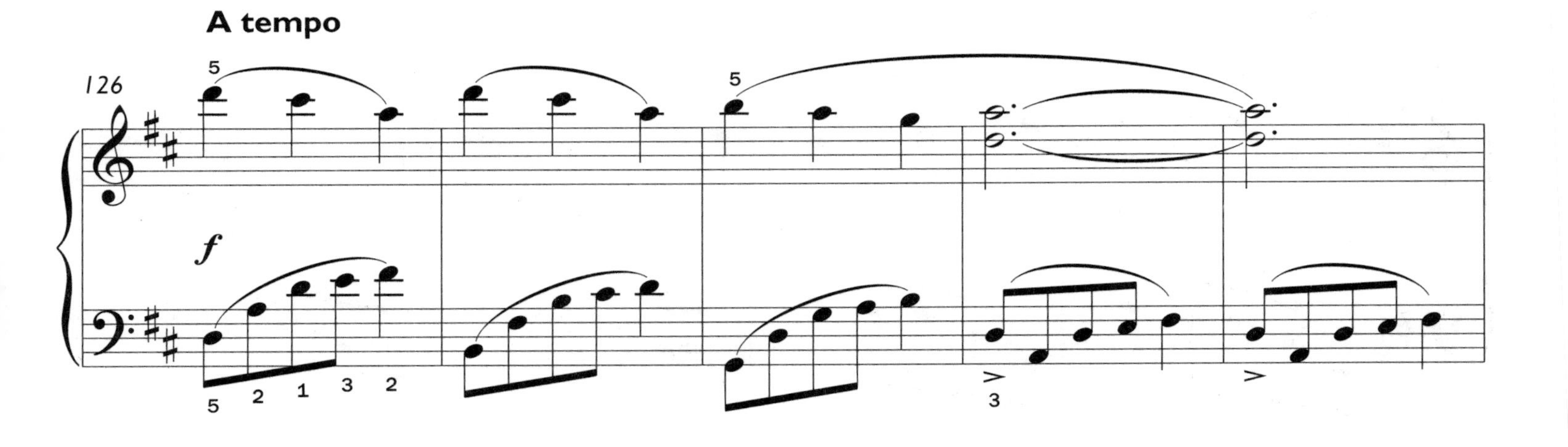
A tempo
126
f

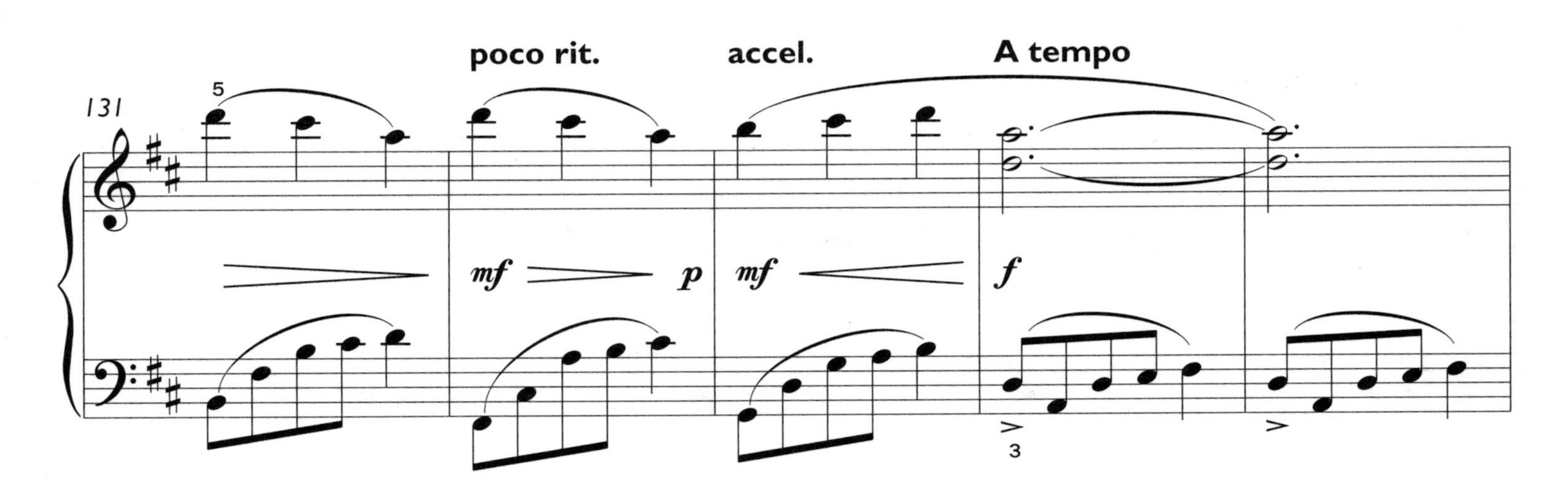
poco rit.
accel.
A tempo
131
mf
p
mf
f

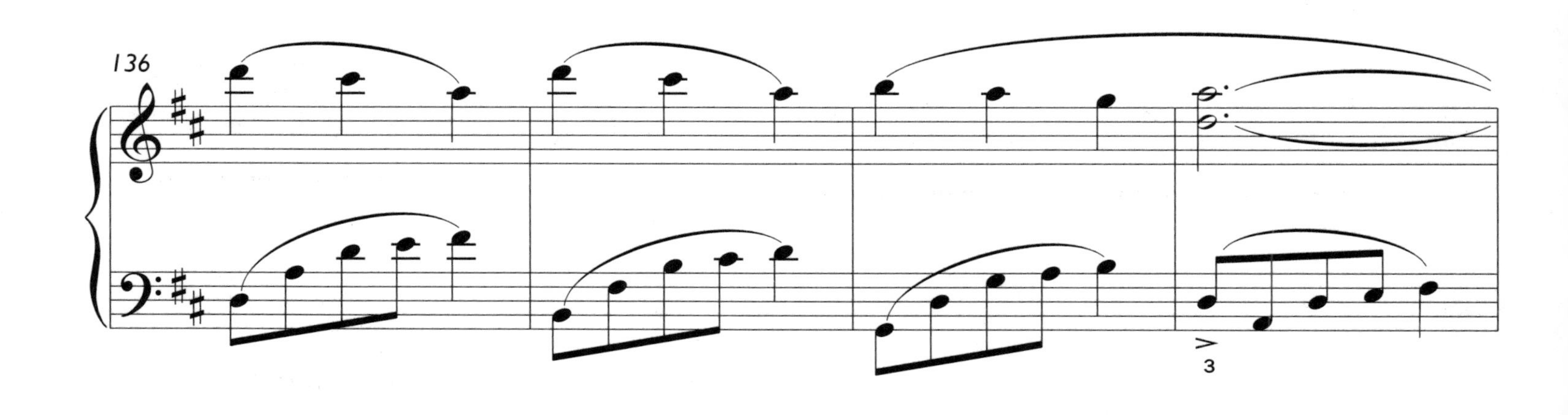
136

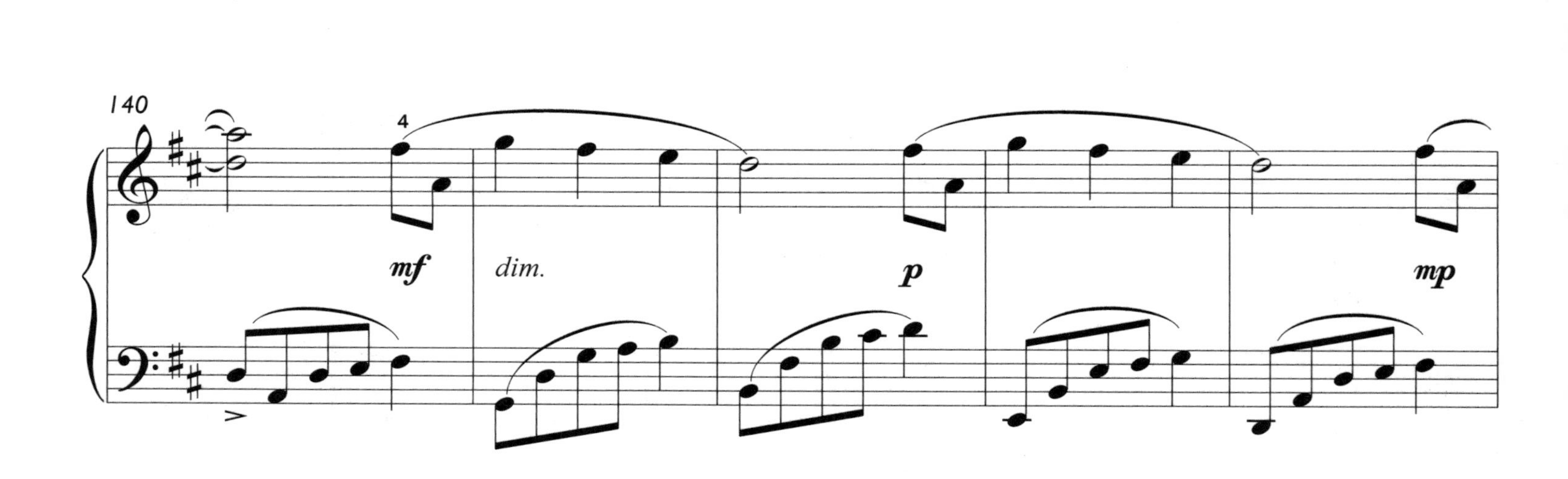
140
mf
dim.
p
mp

145
allarg.
cresc.
f

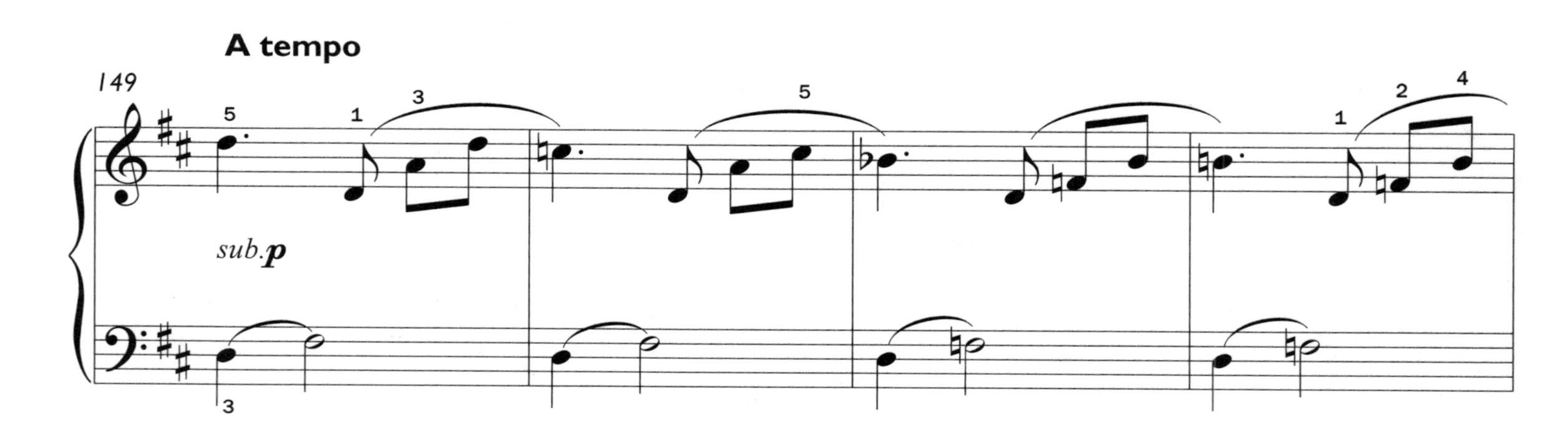
A tempo
149
sub.p

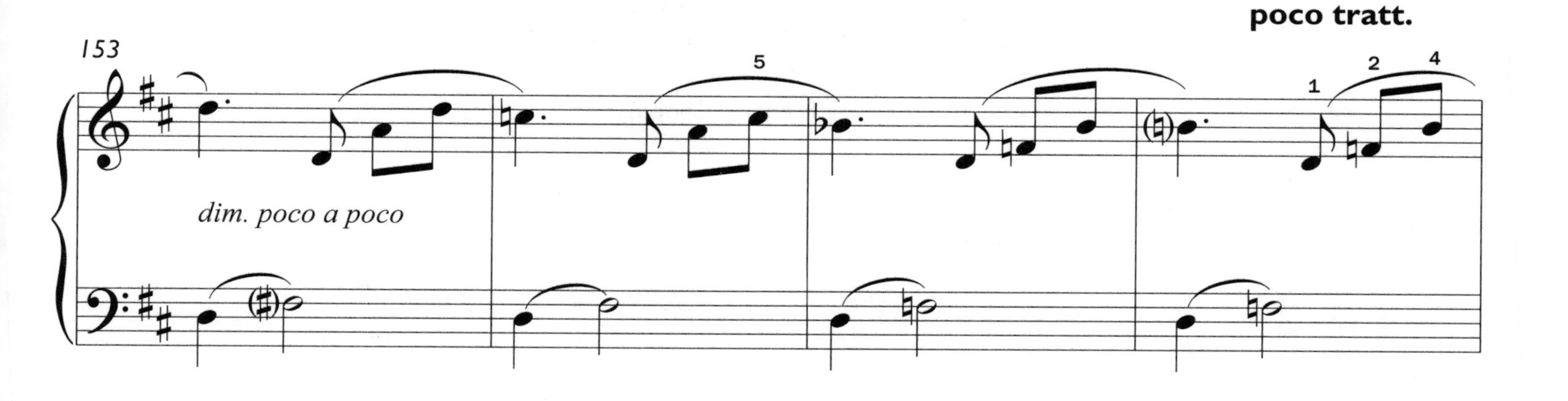
poco tratt.
153
dim. poco a poco

poco tratt.
157
pp

poco tratt.
161

molto rall.
165
pp

'Raindrop' Prelude

Music by Frédéric Chopin

rit.
A tempo
dim.

Casablanca

(As Time Goes By)

Words & Music by Herman Hupfeld

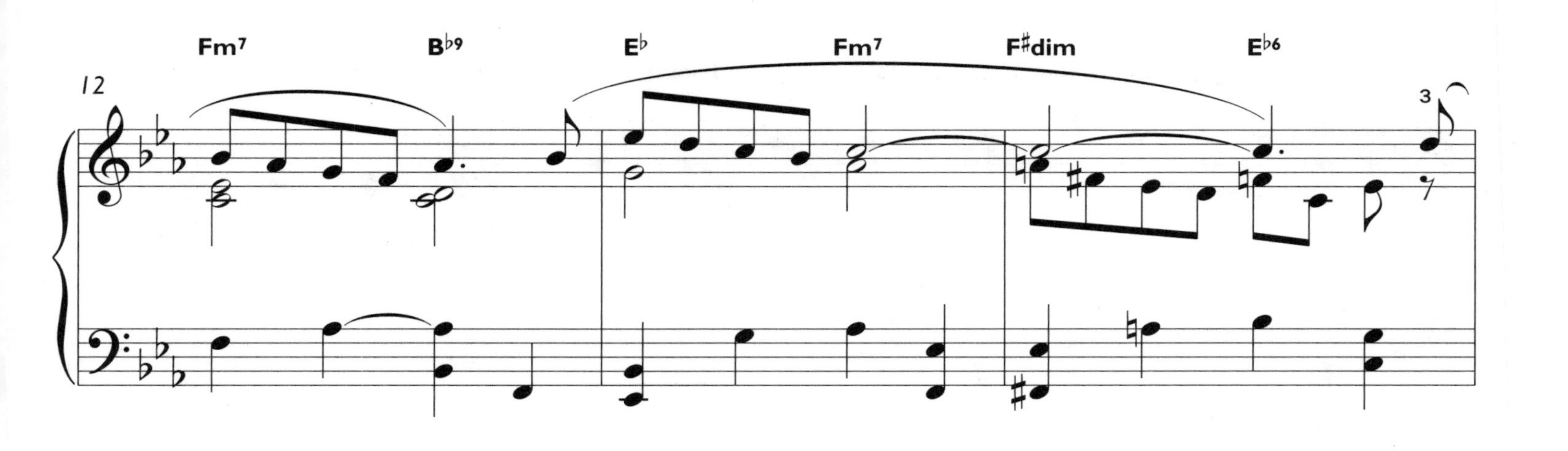
12
Fm7
B♭9
E♭
Fm7
F♯dim
E♭6

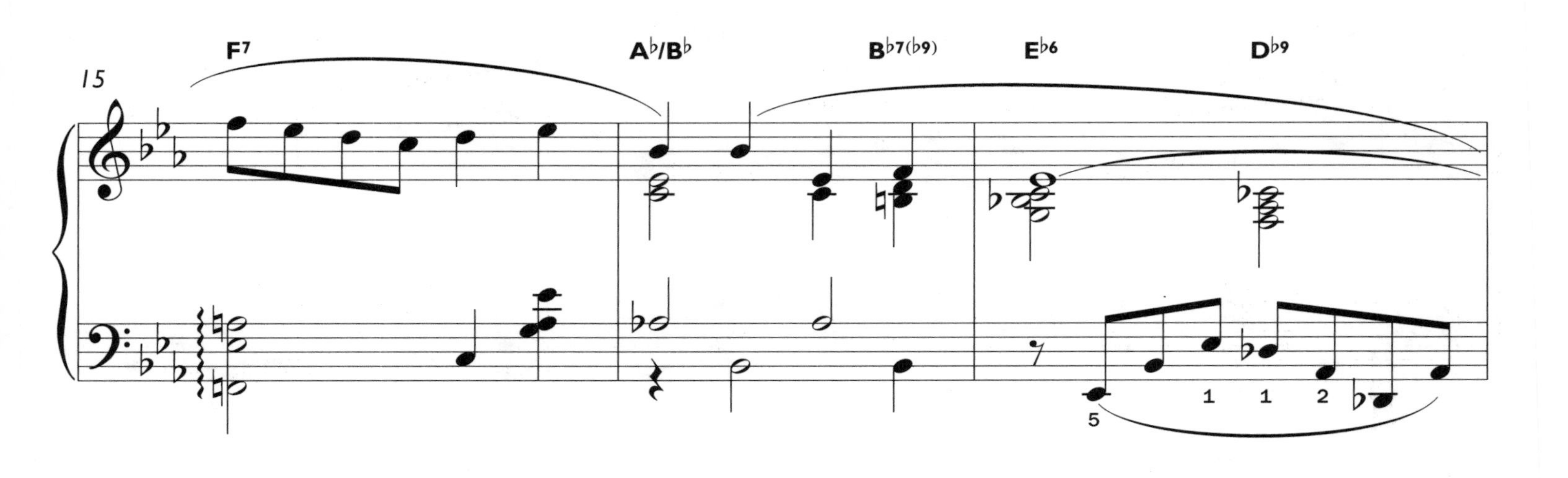
15
F7
A♭/B♭
B♭7(♭9)
E♭6
D♭9

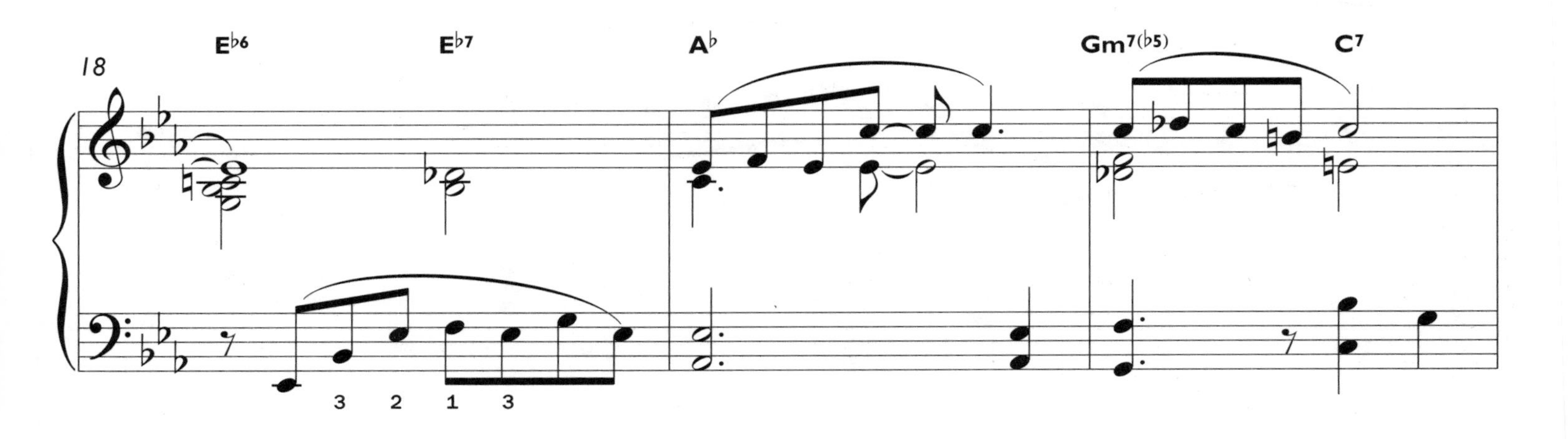
18
E♭6
E♭7
A♭
Gm7(♭5)
C7

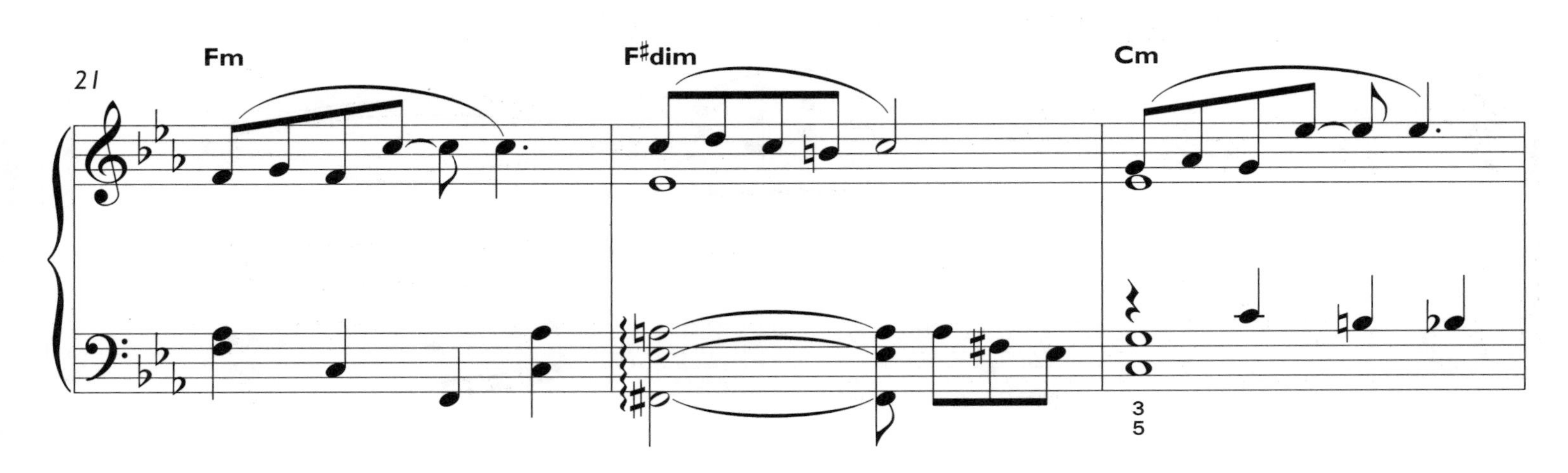
21
Fm
F♯dim
Cm

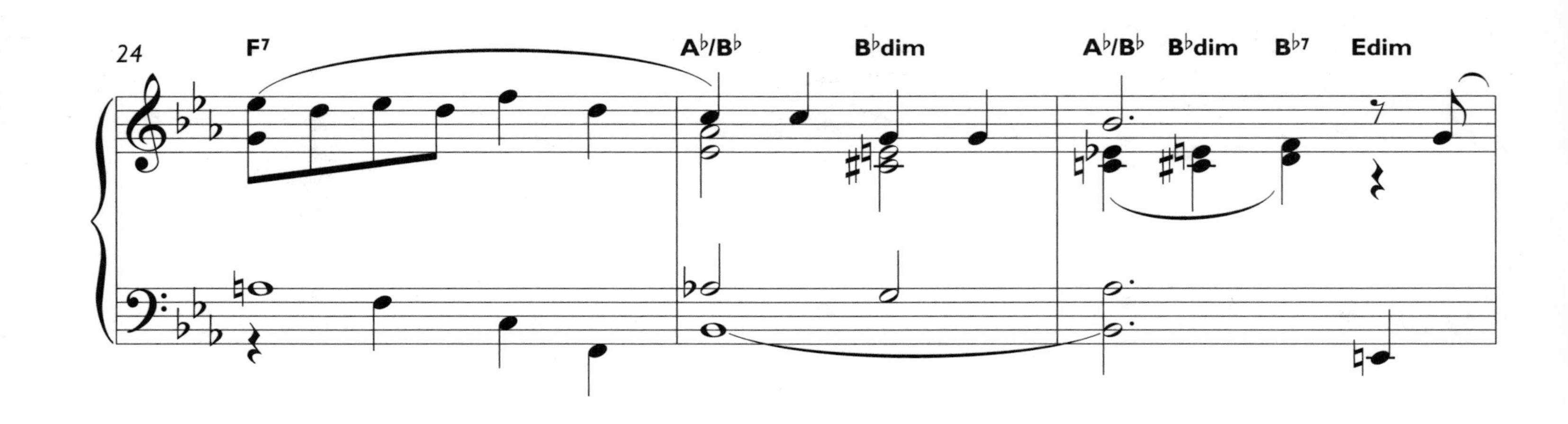

24
F7
A♭/B♭
B♭dim
A♭/B♭
B♭dim
B♭7
Edim

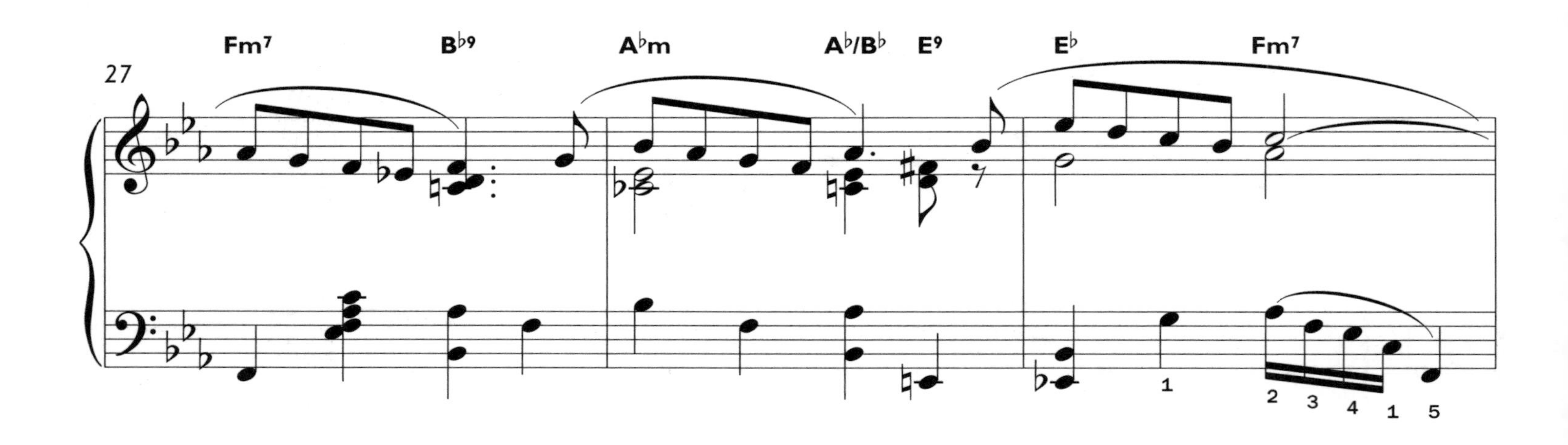

27
Fm7
B♭9
A♭m
A♭/B♭
E9
E♭
Fm7
1
2 3 4 1 5

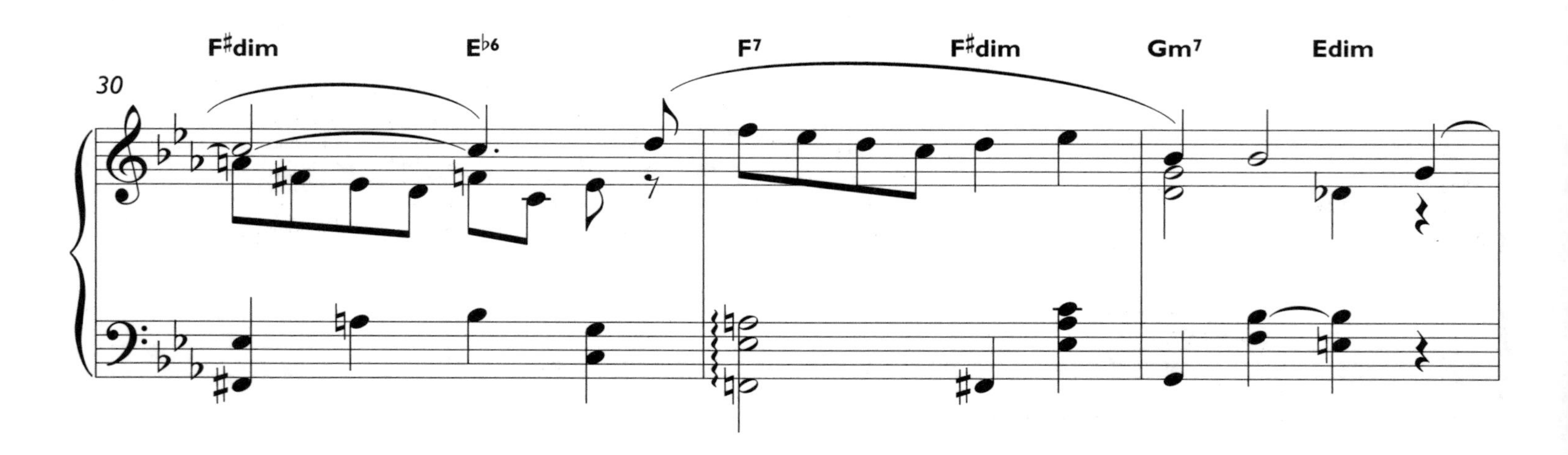

30
F♯dim
E♭6
F7
F♯dim
Gm7
Edim

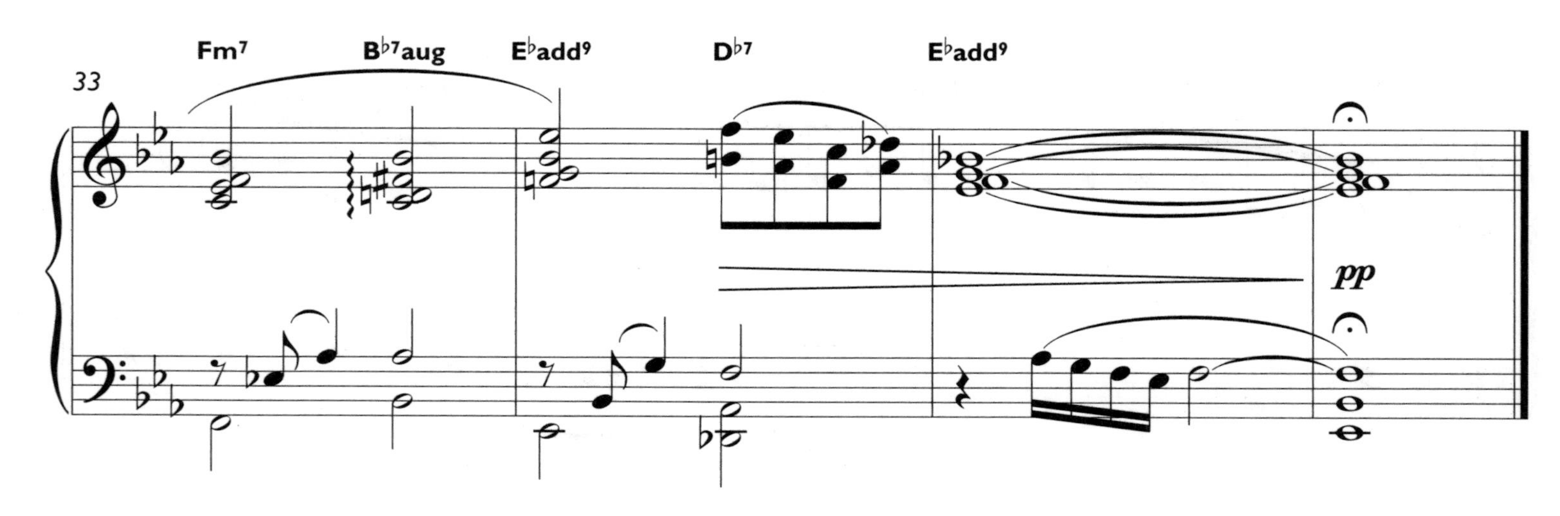

33
Fm7
B♭7aug
E♭add9
D♭7
E♭add9
pp

The Lord Of The Rings: The Return Of The King

(Into The West)

Words & Music by Annie Lennox, Howard Shore & Fran Walsh

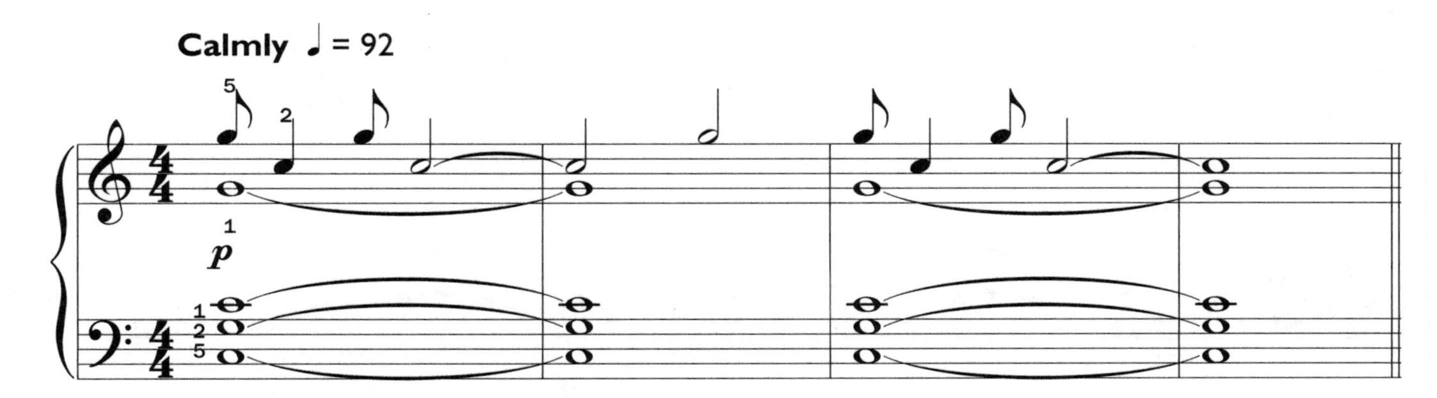

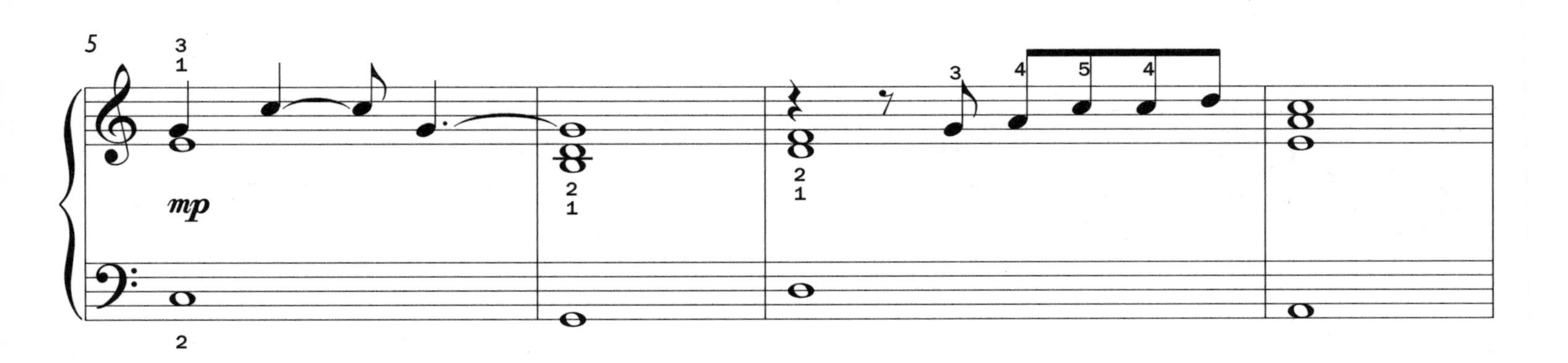

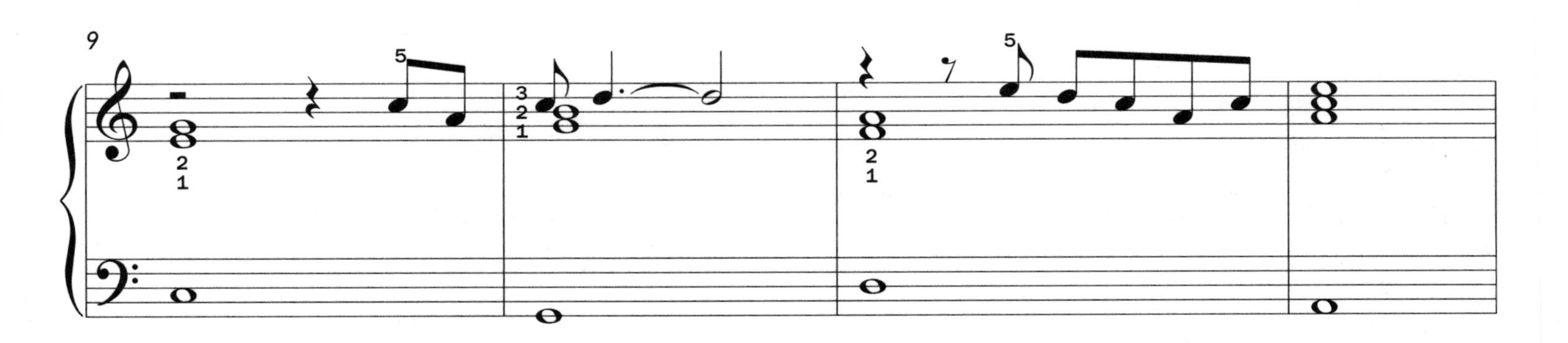

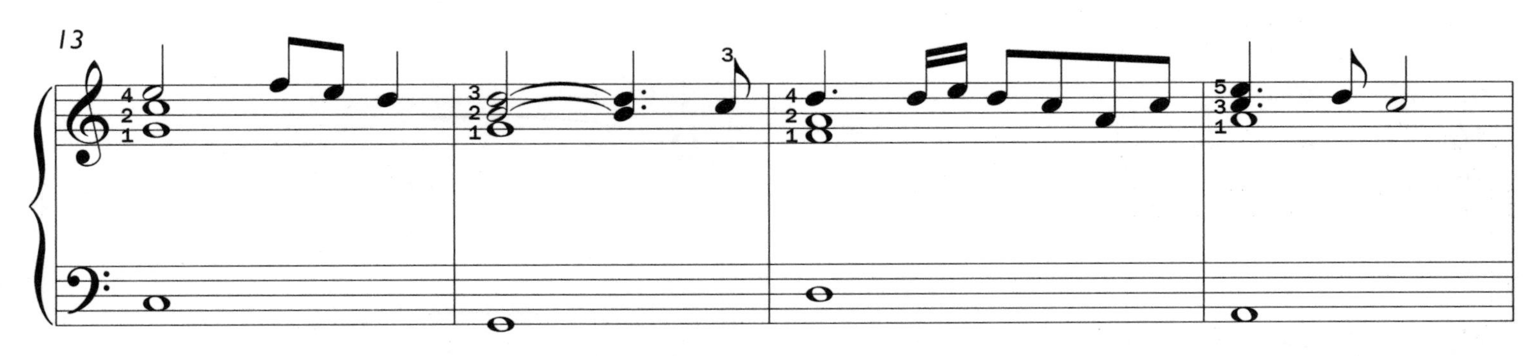

cresc.
mf cresc.
f

dim.

Casino Royale

(Vesper)

Music by David Arnold

13
mf
16

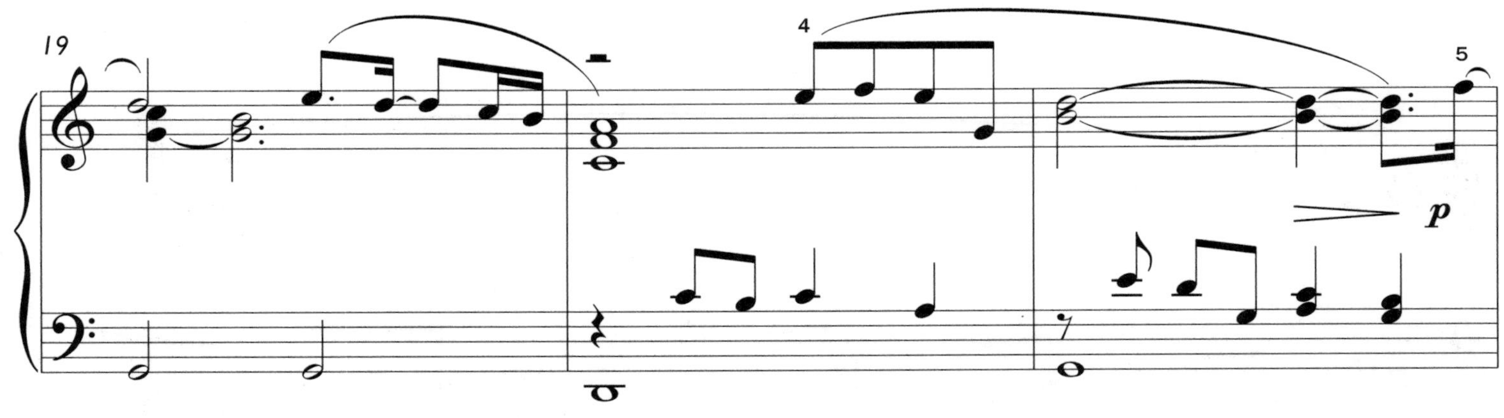
19
p

22
dim.

Pride And Prejudice

(Leaving Netherfield)

Music by Dario Marianelli

10
A tempo
mp
13
16
rit.
A tempo
19
rit.
2
2
2
2

Schindler's List

(Theme)

Music by John Williams

14
Am6
1
Em
4 1
C7
16
Em
Am7
D7
G
B7
Em
Am7
19
D7
G
F♯m7(♭5)
B7
Em
22
F♯m7(♭5)
B7
Em
D
Am7
B7
25
Em
pp

Don't Know Why

Words & Music by Jesse Harris

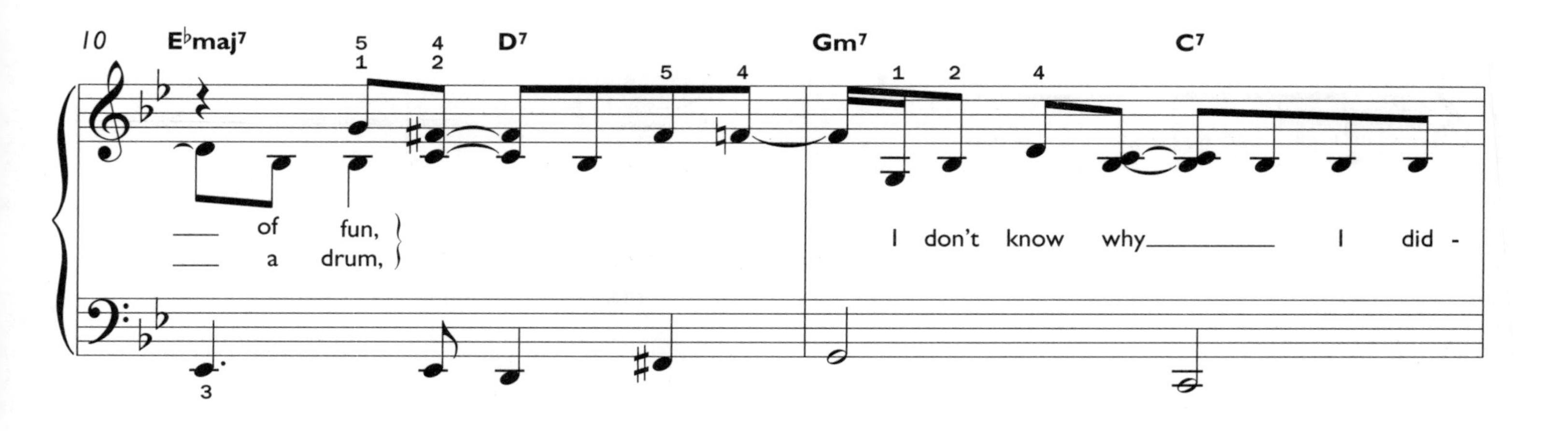
10
E♭maj7
D7
Gm7
C7
___ of fun,
___ a drum,
I don't know why___ I did -

To Coda ⊕

12
F7sus4
B♭
F11
Gm7
C7
F7sus4
B♭
- n't come,___ I
don't know why___ I did - n't
come.

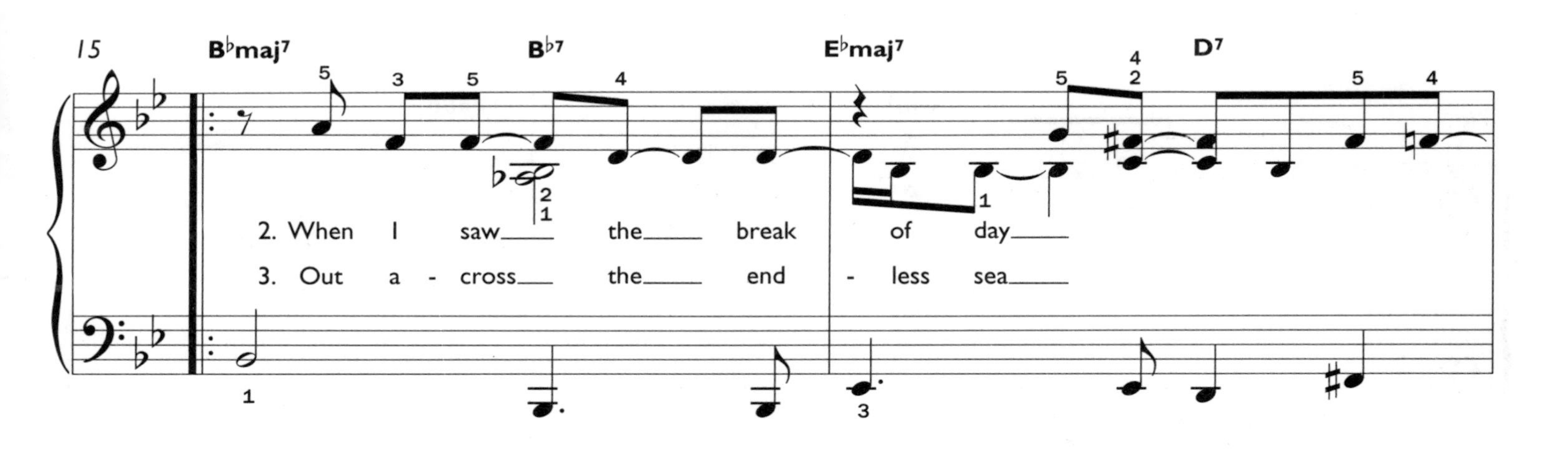
15
B♭maj7
B♭7
E♭maj7
D7
2. When I saw___ the___ break of day___
3. Out a - cross___ the___ end - less sea___

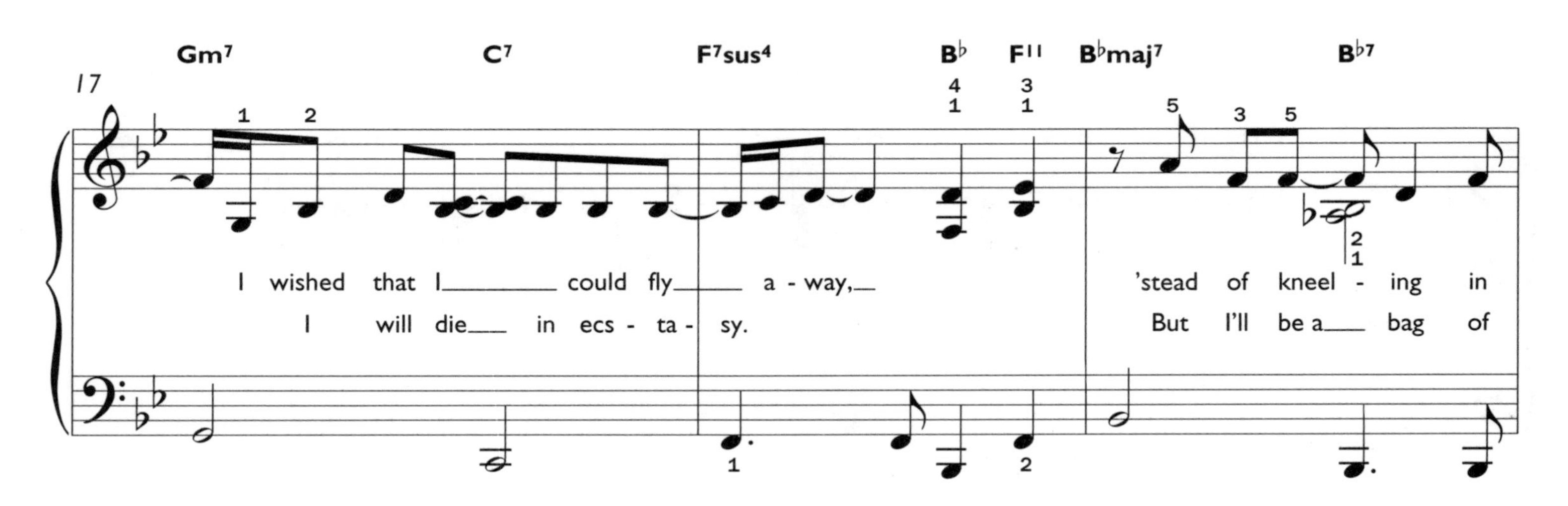
17
Gm7
C7
F7sus4
B♭
F11
B♭maj7
B♭7
I wished that I___ could fly___ a - way,___
I will die___ in ecs - ta - sy.
'stead of kneel - ing in
But I'll be a___ bag of

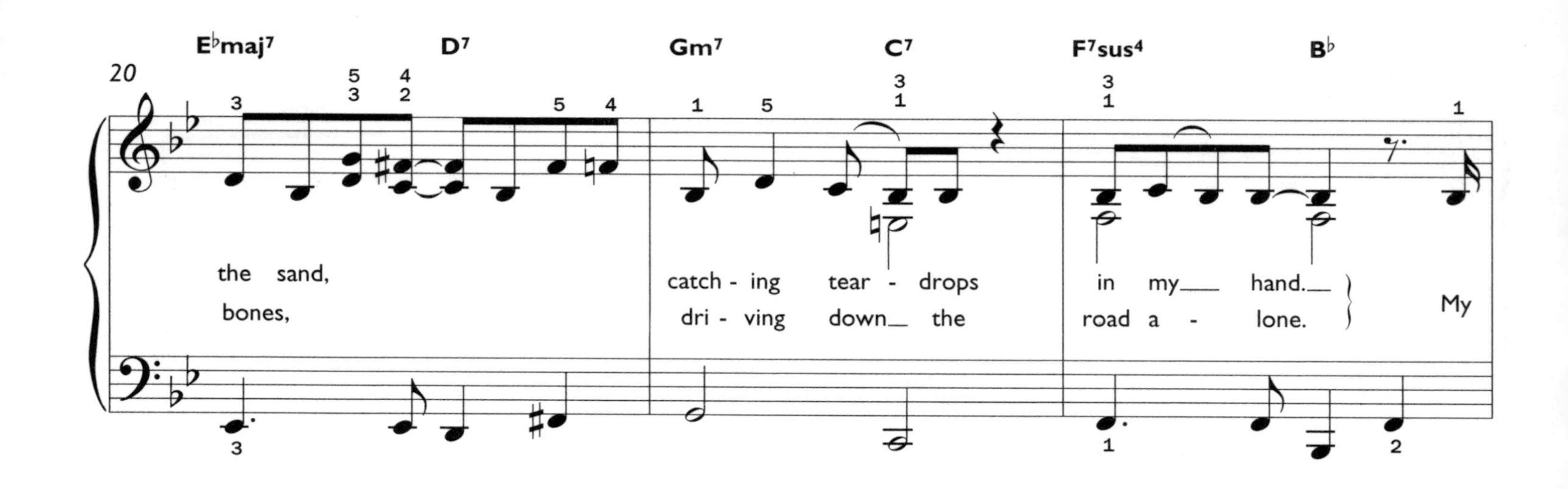
20
E♭maj7
D7
Gm7
C7
F7sus4
B♭
the sand,
catch - ing tear - drops
in my hand.
bones,
dri - ving down the
road a - lone.
My

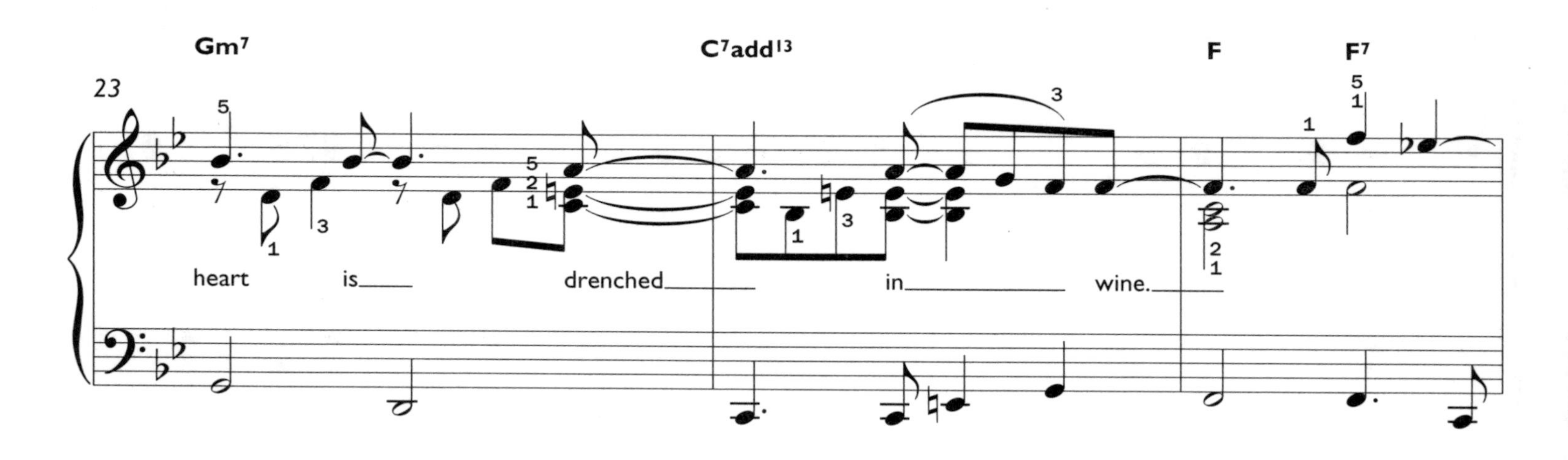
23
Gm7
C7add13
F
F7
heart is drenched in wine.

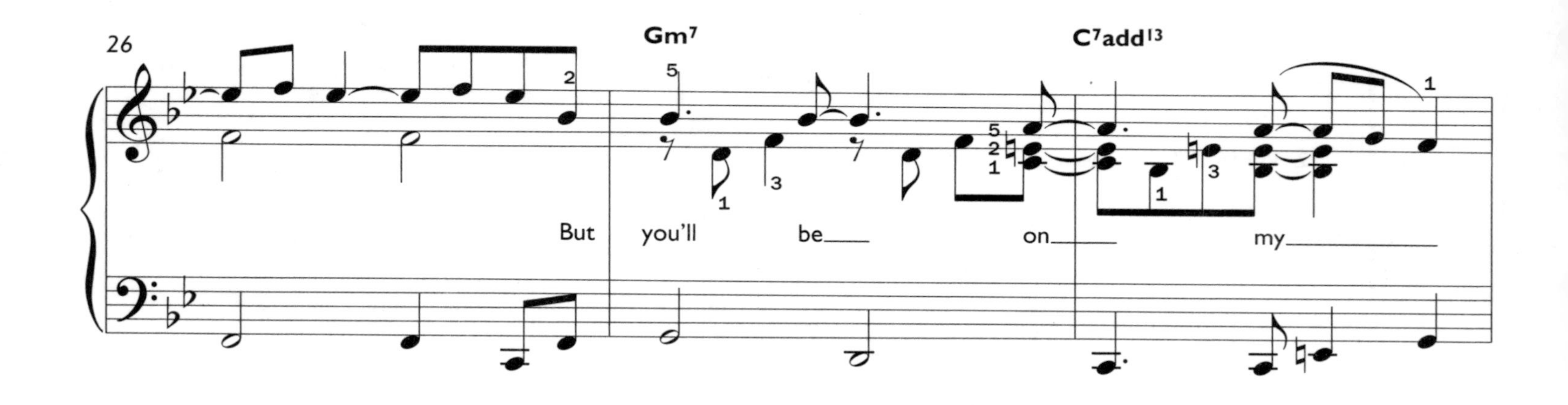
26
Gm7
C7add13
But you'll be on my

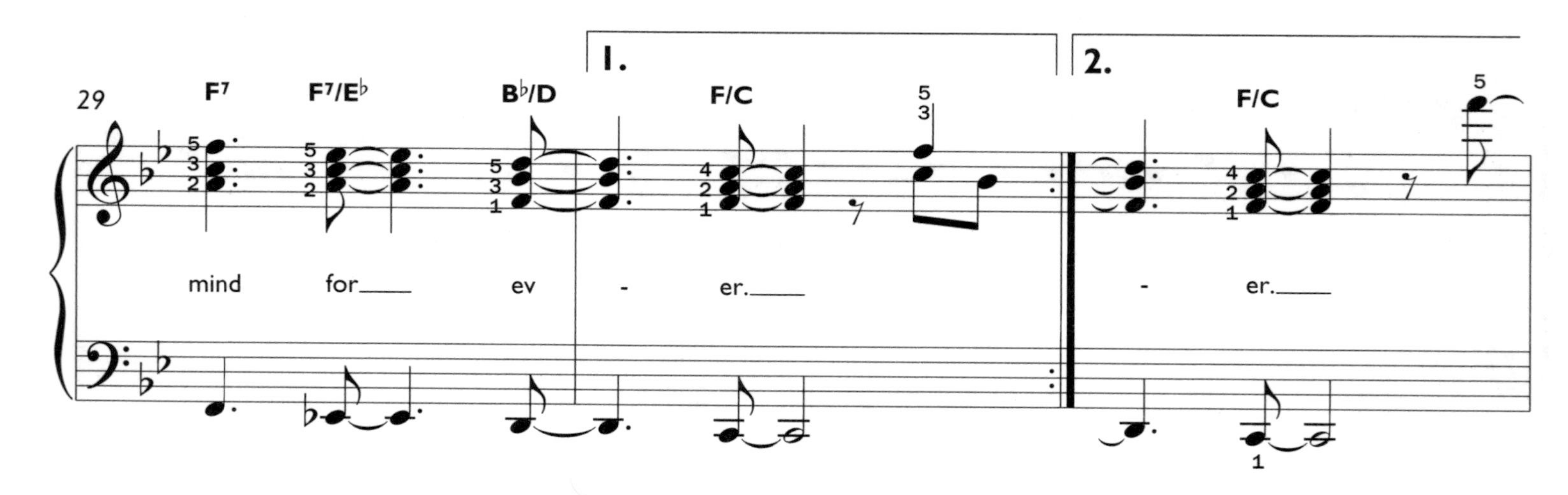
29
1.
2.
F7
F7/E♭
B♭/D
F/C
F/C
mind for ev - er.
- er.

B♭maj7 B♭7 E♭maj7 D7 Gm7 C7
F7sus4 B♭maj7 B♭7
E♭maj7 D7 Gm7 C7 F7sus4
D.S. al Coda
Coda
Gm7 C7 F7sus4 B♭ B♭/F
don't know why I did - n't come. I
Gm7 C7 F7sus4 B♭
don't know why I did - n't come.

Fever

Words & Music by John Davenport & Eddie Cooley

13
when you kiss me, fe - ver when you hold__ me tight.

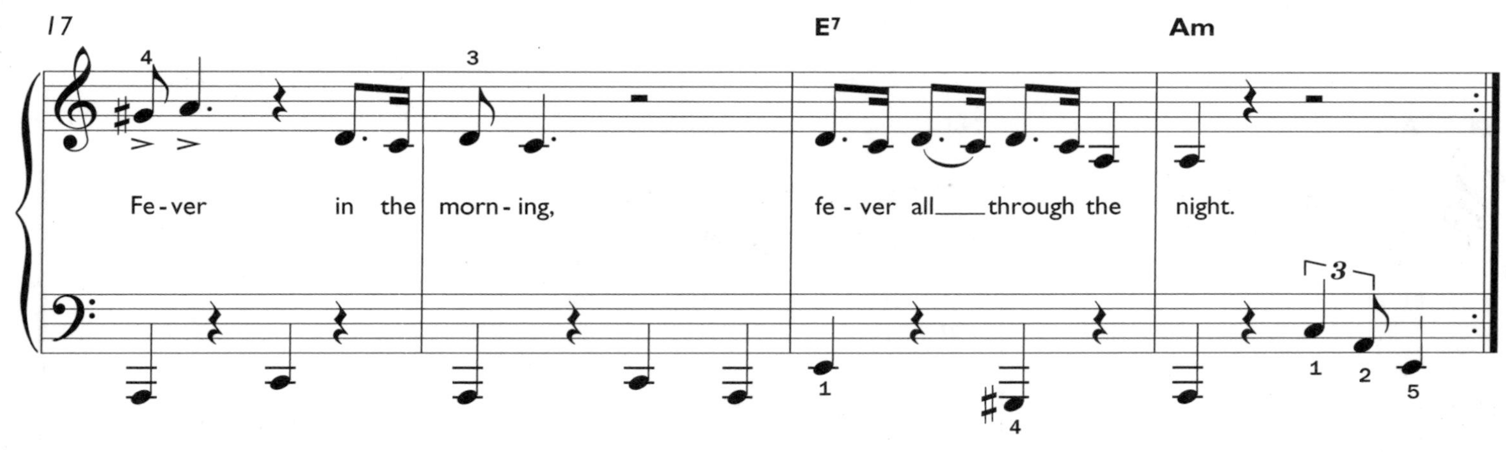
17
1, 3, 4.
E7
Am
Fe-ver in the morn-ing, fe - ver all__through the night.

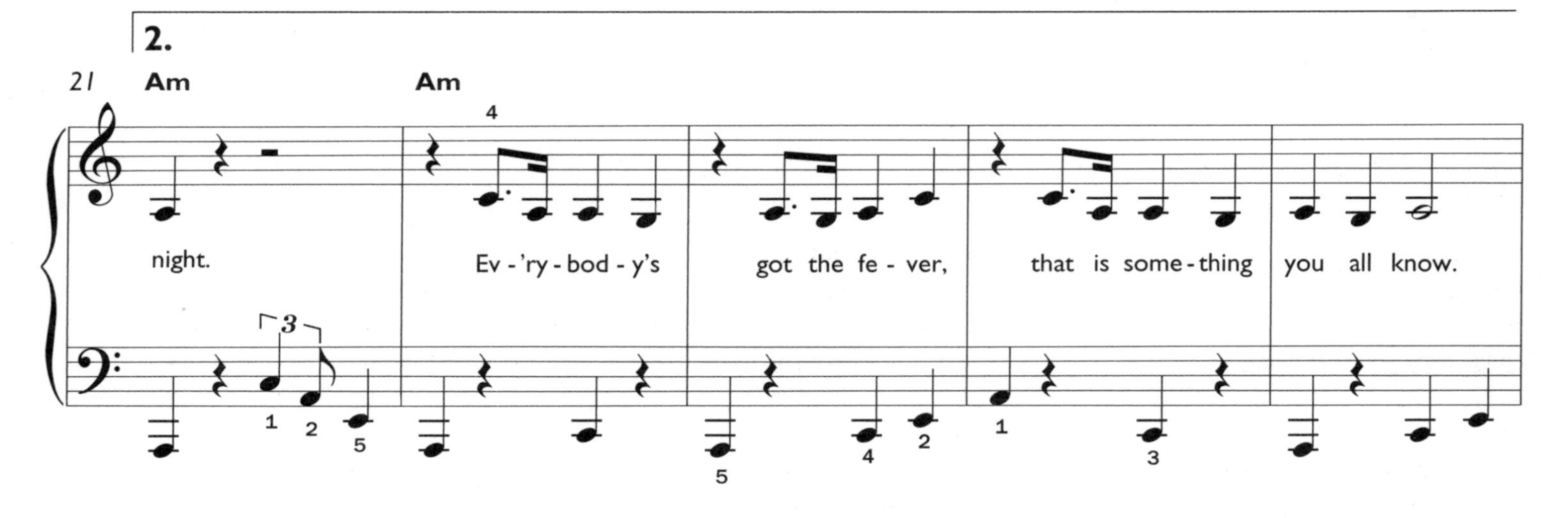
2.
21
Am
Am
night. Ev - 'ry - bod - y's got the fe - ver, that is some - thing you all know.

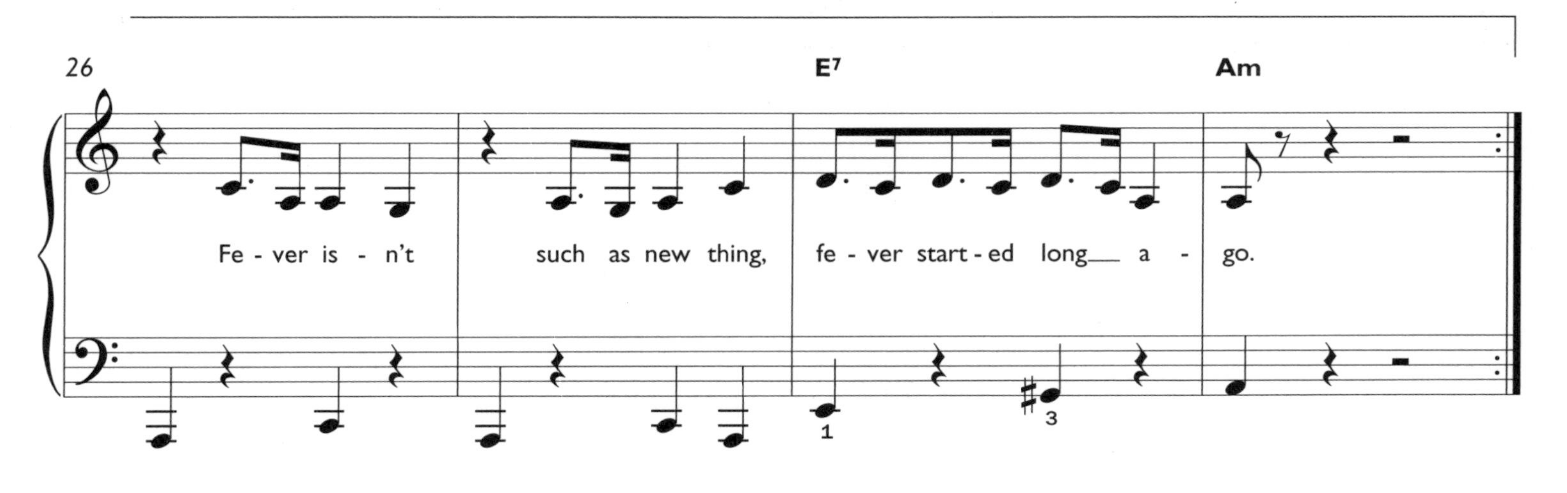
26
E7
Am
Fe - ver is - n't such as new thing, fe - ver start - ed long__ a - go.

Verse 3:
Romeo loved Juliet,
Juliet she felt the same;
When he put his arms around her, he said,
"Julie, baby you're my flame."

Chorus:
Thou givest fever, when we kisseth
Fever with thy flaming youth;
Fever, I'm afire
Fever, yeah I burn forsooth.

Verse 4:
Captain Smith and Pocahontas
Had a very mad affair,
When her Daddy tried to kill him, she said,
"Daddy Oh, don't you dare."

Chorus:
He gives me fever, with his kisses,
Fever when he holds me tight.
Fever - I'm his Missus
Oh Daddy won't you treat him right.

Verse 5:
Now you've listened to my story
Here's the point that I have made:
Chicks were born to give you fever
Be it Fahrenheit or centigrade.

Chorus:
They give you fever, when you kiss them,
Fever if you live you learn.
Fever - till you sizzle
What a lovely way to burn.

Lullaby Of Birdland

Words by George David Weiss
Music by George Shearing

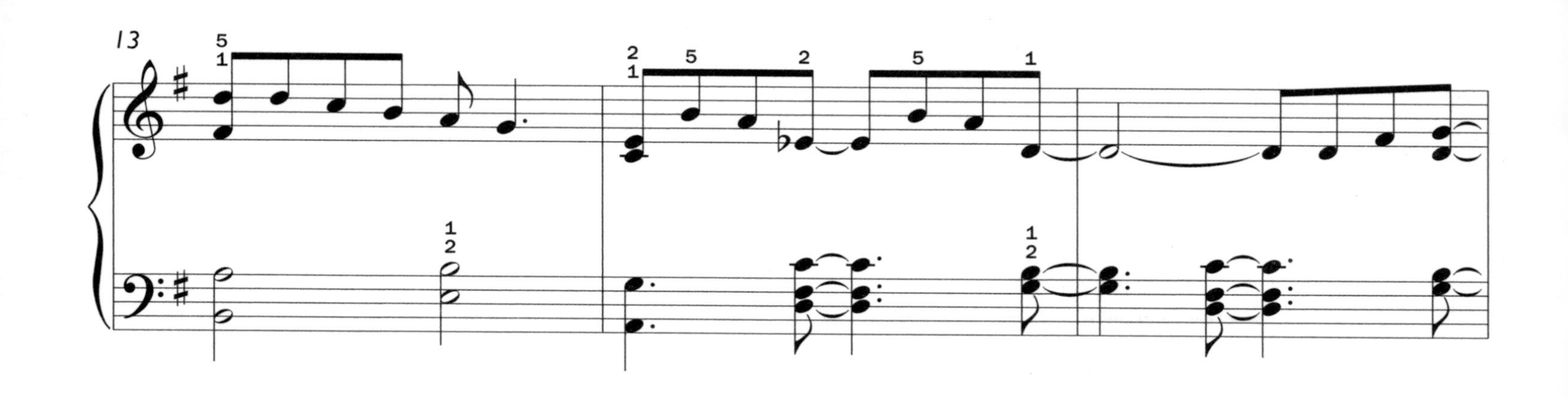
13

16

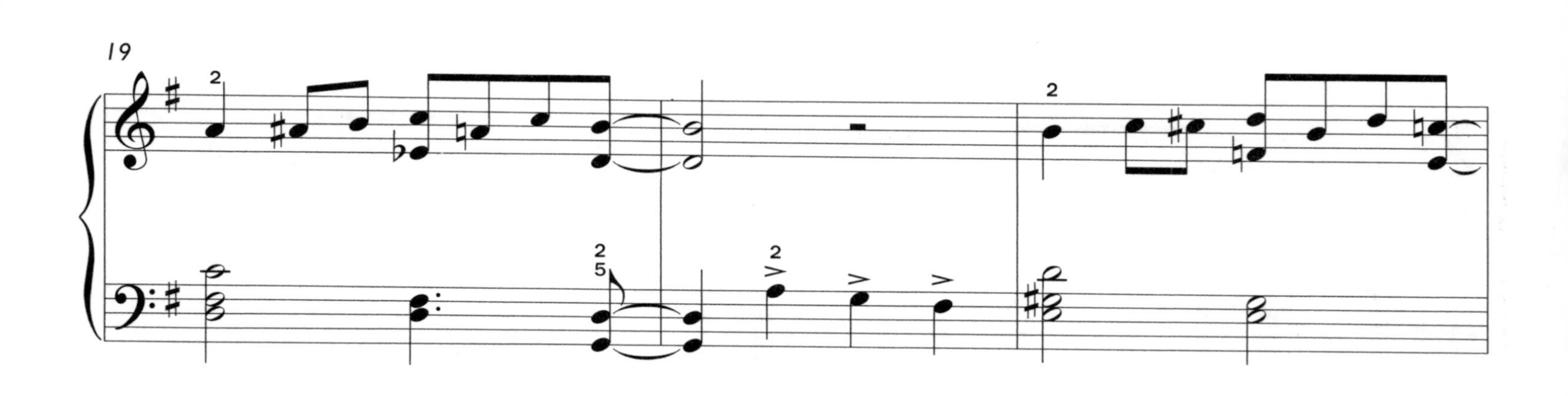
19

22

25

28

31
1.
2.

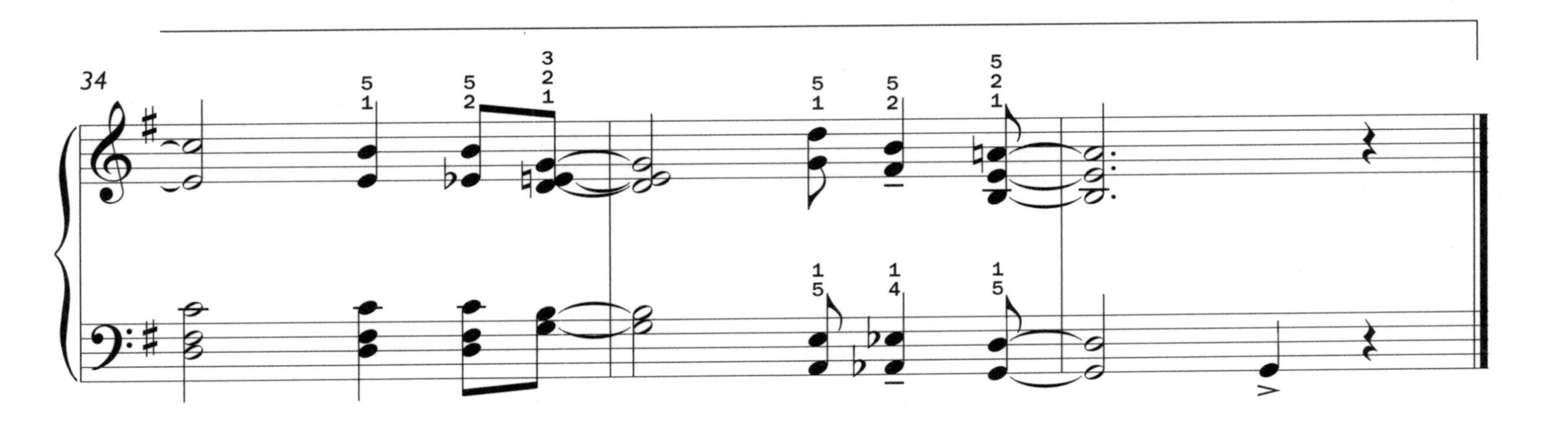
34

Georgia On My Mind

Words by Stuart Gorrell
Music by Hoagy Carmichael

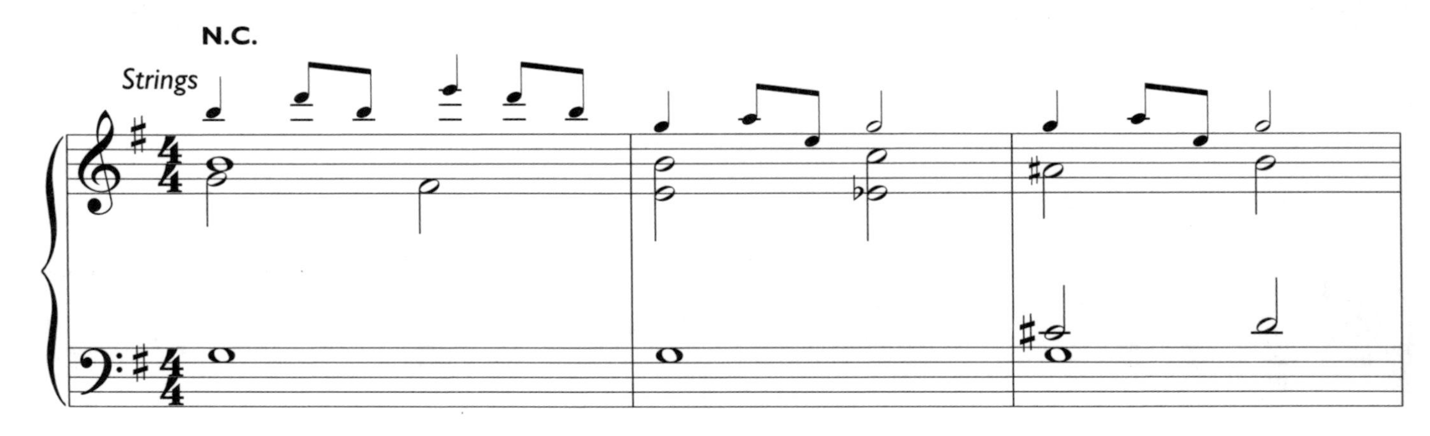

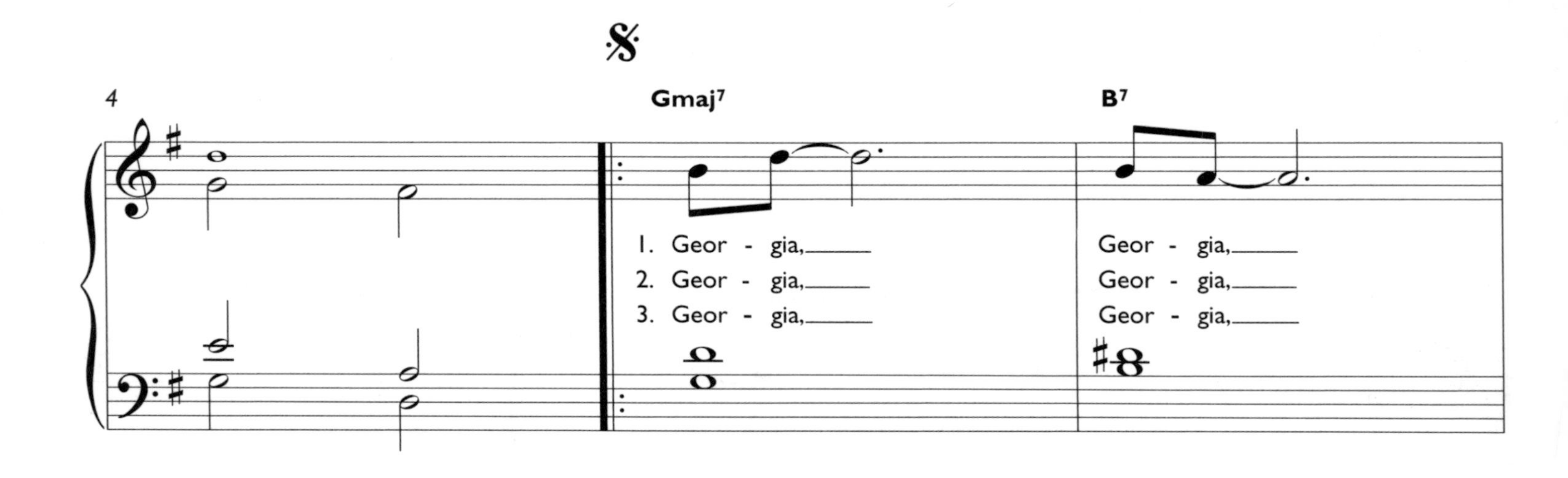

1.
10
A7
D9
D7•♭9
B7♭5
E9
A7
D7•♭9
Geor - gia on my mind.

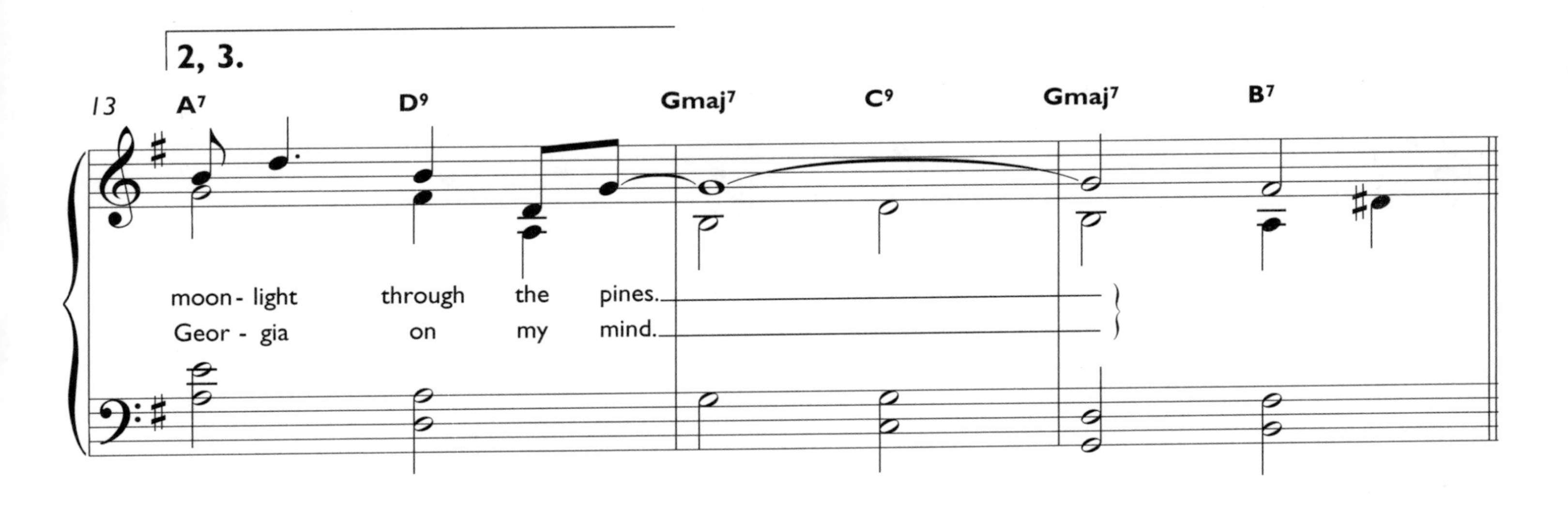
2, 3.
13
A7
D9
Gmaj7
C9
Gmaj7
B7
moon- light through the pines.
Geor - gia on my mind.

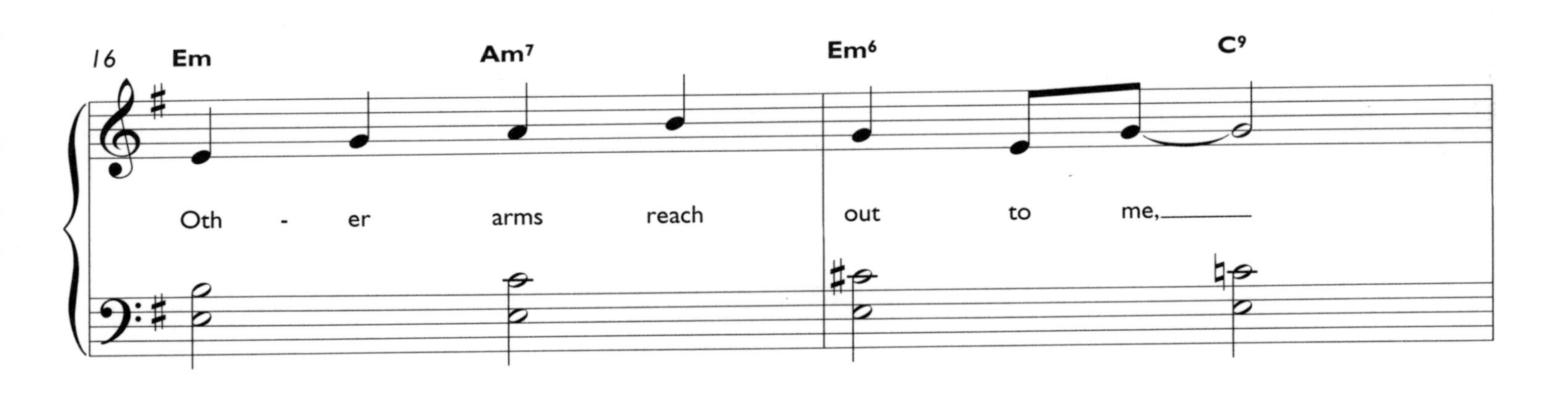
16
Em
Am7
Em6
C9
Oth - er arms reach out to me,

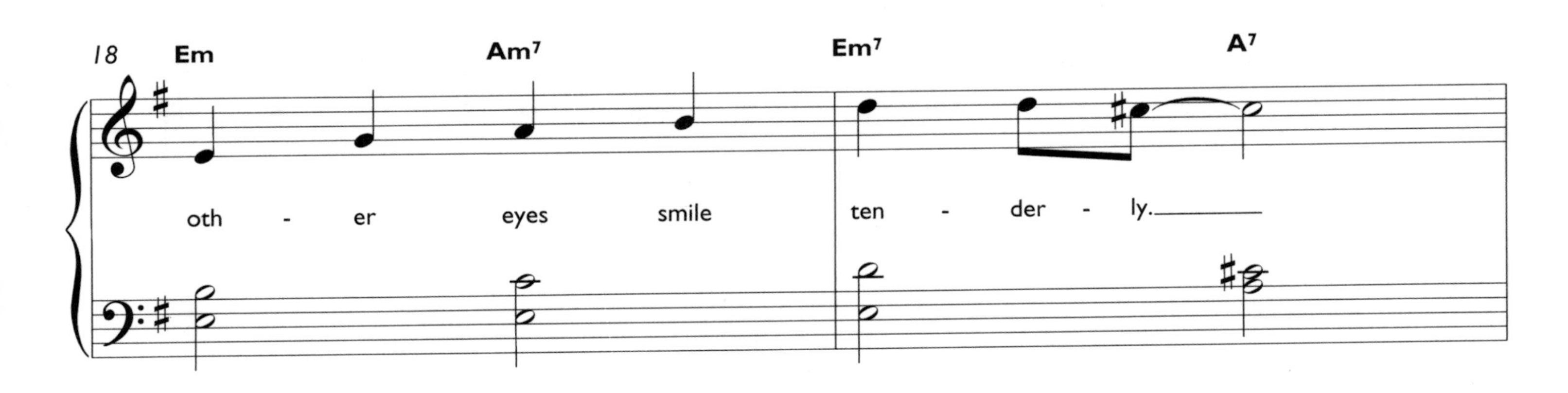
18
Em
Am7
Em7
A7
oth - er eyes smile ten - der - ly.

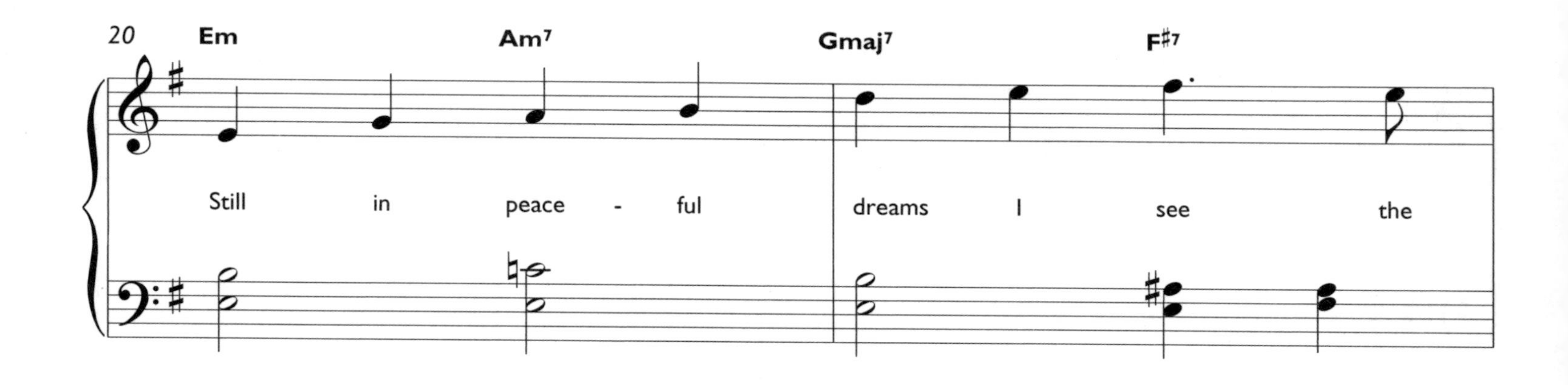
20
Em
Am7
Gmaj7
F♯7
Still in peace - ful
dreams I see the

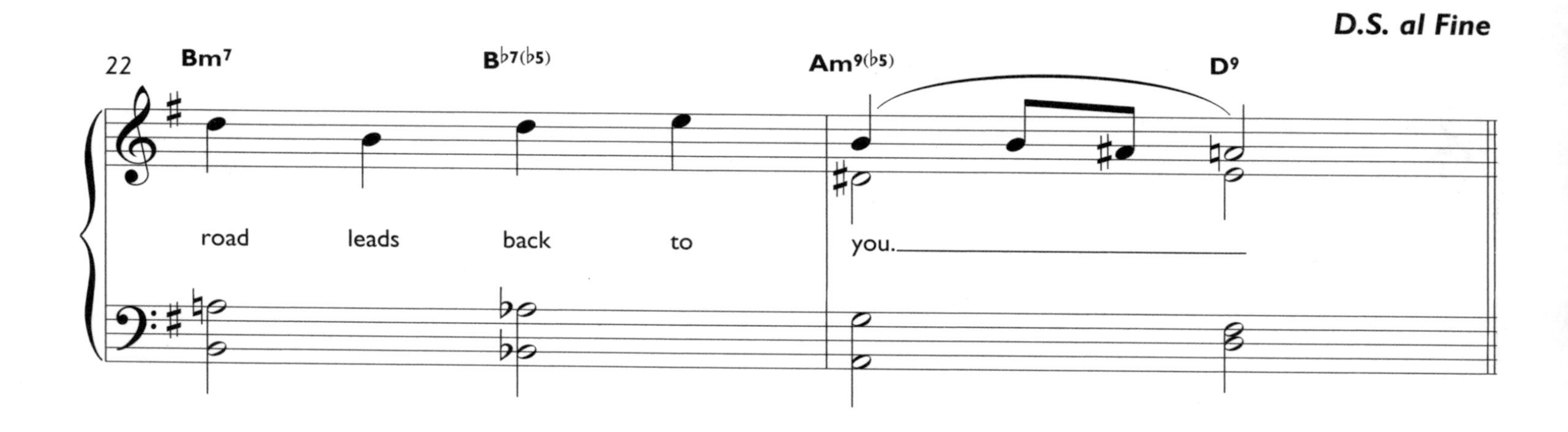
D.S. al Fine
22
Bm7
B♭7(♭5)
Am9(♭5)
D9
road leads back to
you.

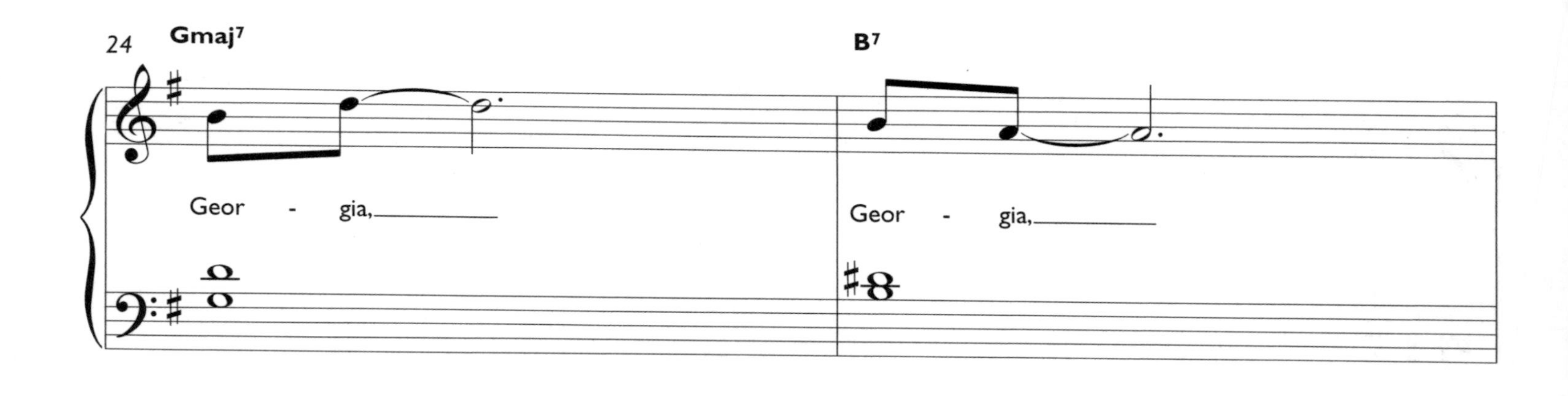
24
Gmaj7
B7
Geor - gia,
Geor - gia,

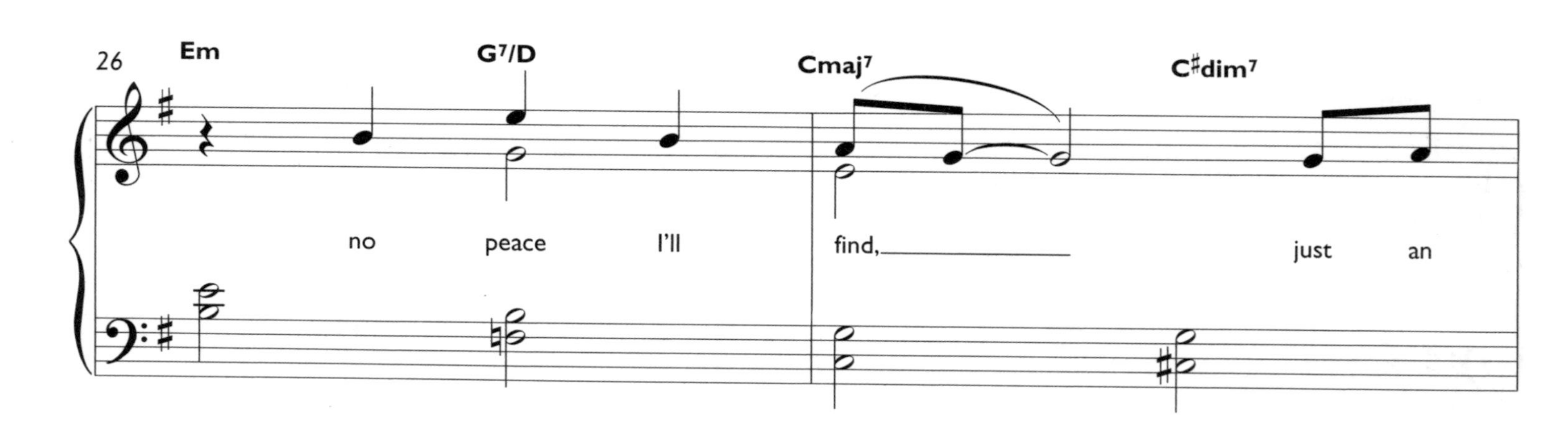
26
Em
G7/D
Cmaj7
C♯dim7
no peace I'll
find,
just an

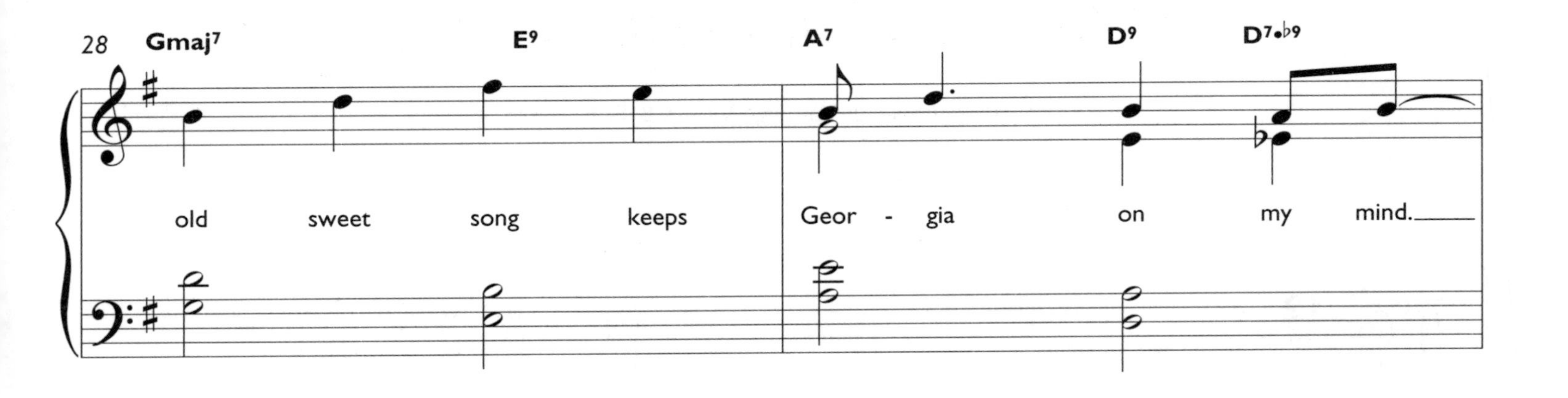
28
Gmaj7
E9
A7
D9
D7♭9
old sweet song keeps Geor - gia on my mind.

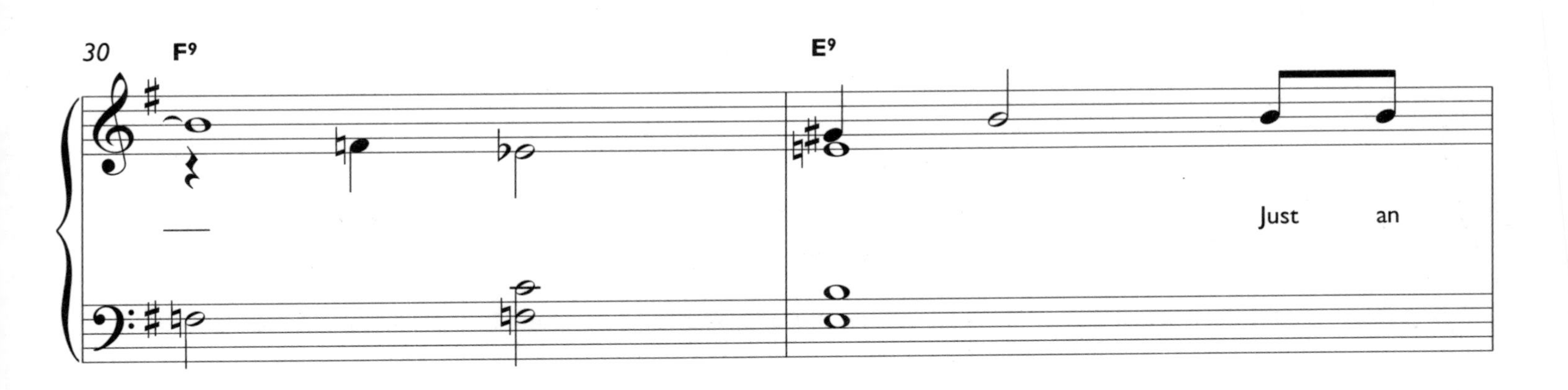
30
F9
E9
Just an

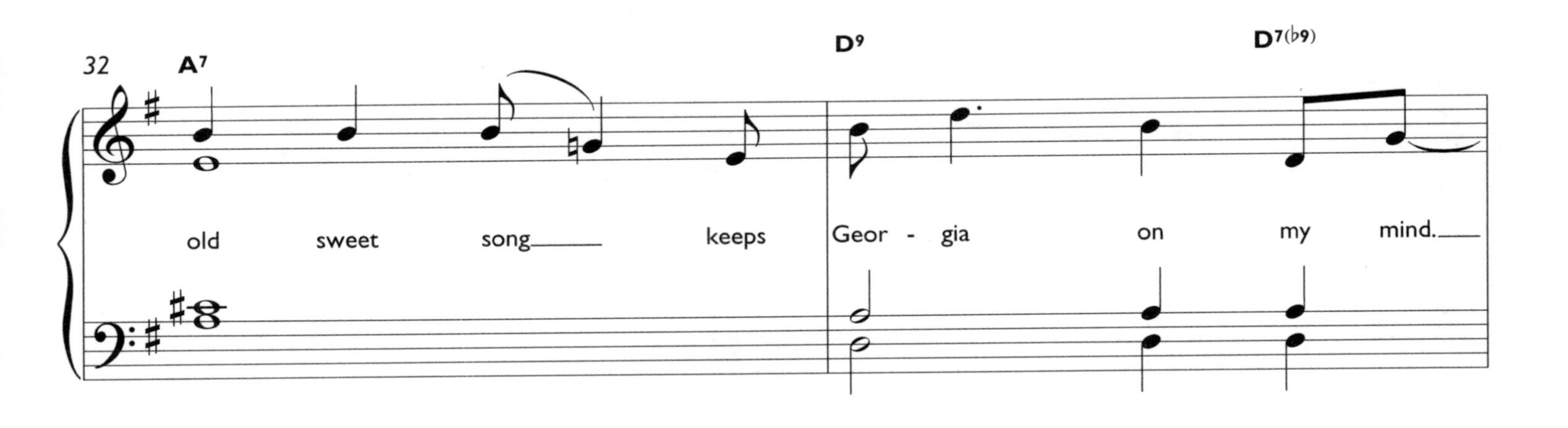
32
A7
D9
D7(♭9)
old sweet song keeps Geor - gia on my mind.

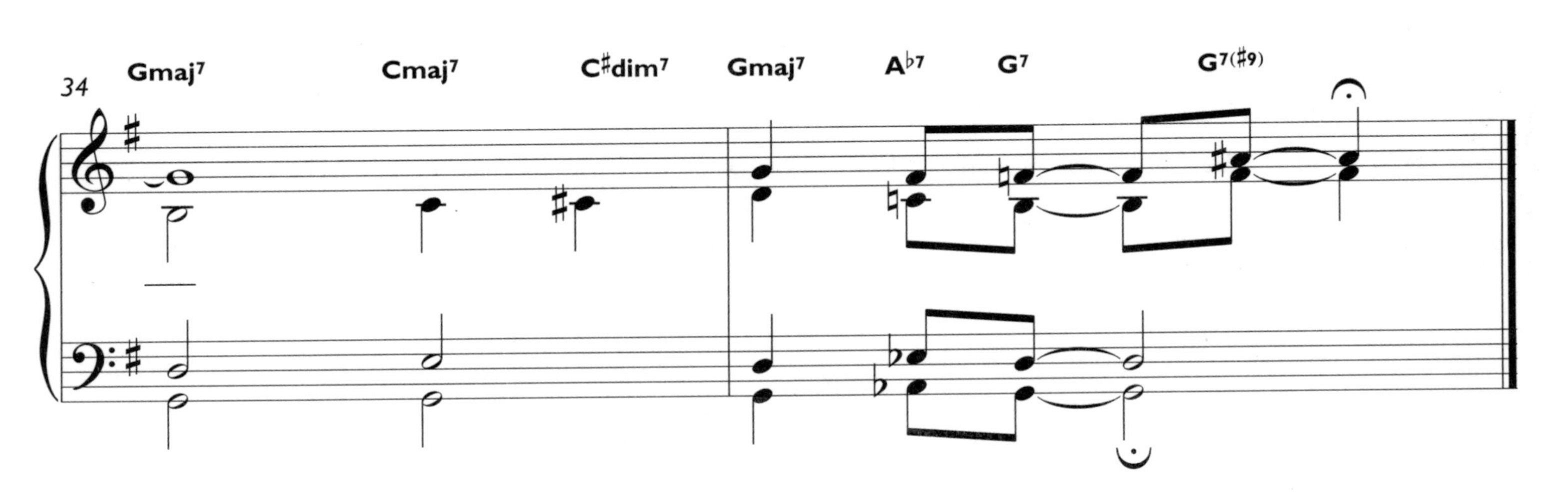
34
Gmaj7
Cmaj7
C♯dim7
Gmaj7
A♭7
G7
G7(♯9)

What A Wonderful World

Words & Music by George Weiss & Bob Thiele

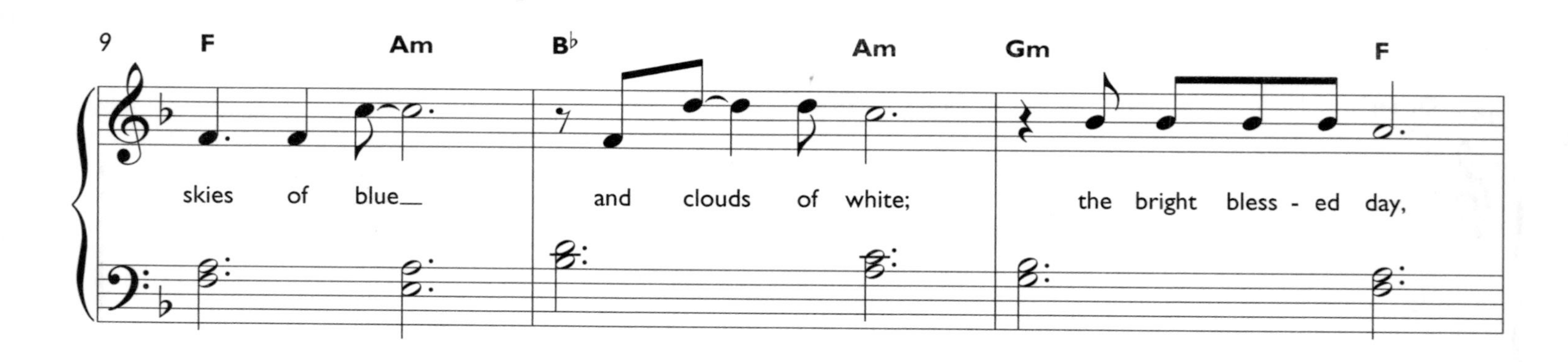

12
A7 Dm D♭
the dark sa - cred night. And I think to my - self,
14
Gm7 C7 F Gm7/F Gm Fmaj7
2
what a won - der - ful world. The
17
B♭6 C/E F
co - lours of the rain - bow, so pret - ty in the sky, are
19
B♭6 C/E F
4
al - so on the fa - ces of peo - ple go - ing by. I see
21
Dm C/E F C
friends shak - ing hands, say - ing "How do you do?"

23
Dm
F♯dim
Gm7
C
C7
They're real - ly say - ing "I love you." I hear
25
F
Am
B♭
Am
Gm
F
ba - bies cry - ing, I watch them grow. They'll learn much more
28
A7
Dm
D♭
Gm7
C7
2
2
than I'll ev - er know. And I think to my - self, what a won - der - ful world.
31
F
E♭(♭5)
D
D7
Gm7
Yes, I think to my - self,
34
C7(♭9)
F
what a won - der - ful world. Oh, yes.

Angie

Words & Music by Mick Jagger & Keith Richards

10
Dm
Am
C
F
G
mon - ey in our coats,
you can't say we're sat - is - fied.
all go up in smoke.
Let me whis - per in your ear.
But

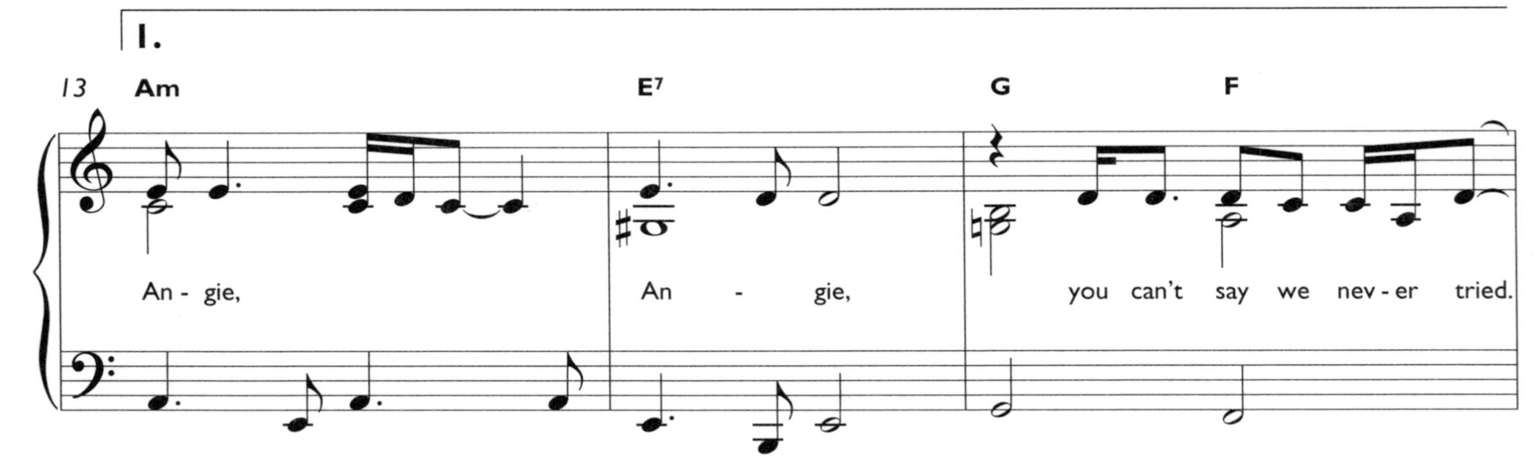
1.
13
Am
E7
G
F
An - gie,
An - gie,
you can't say we nev - er tried.

2.
16
C
Dm
Am
An - gie I still love you ba - by

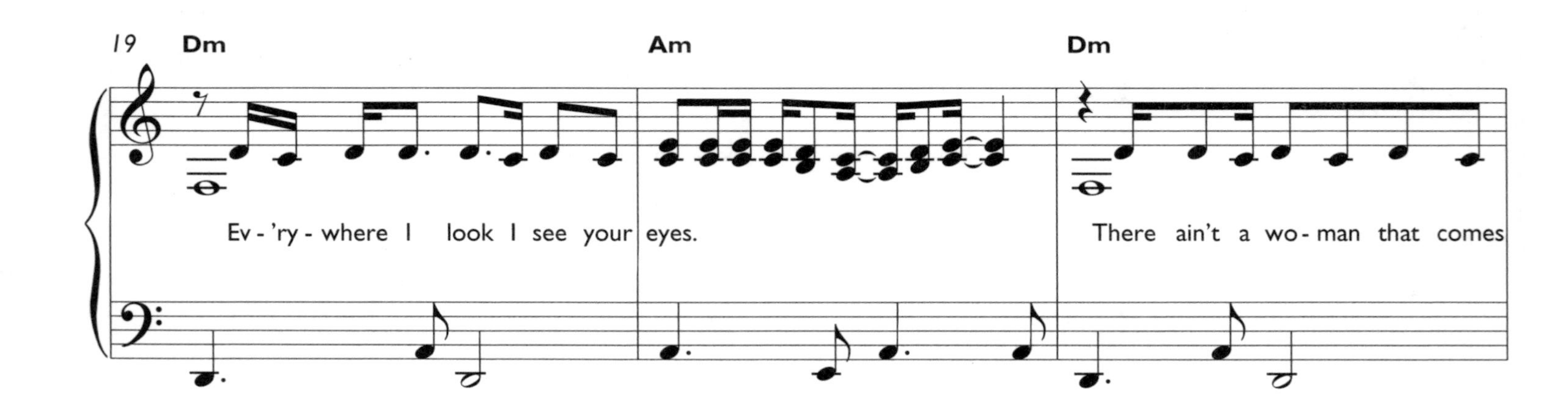
19
Dm
Am
Dm
Ev - 'ry - where I look I see your eyes.
There ain't a wo - man that comes

22
Am
C
F
G
close to you.
Come on ba - by dry your eyes.

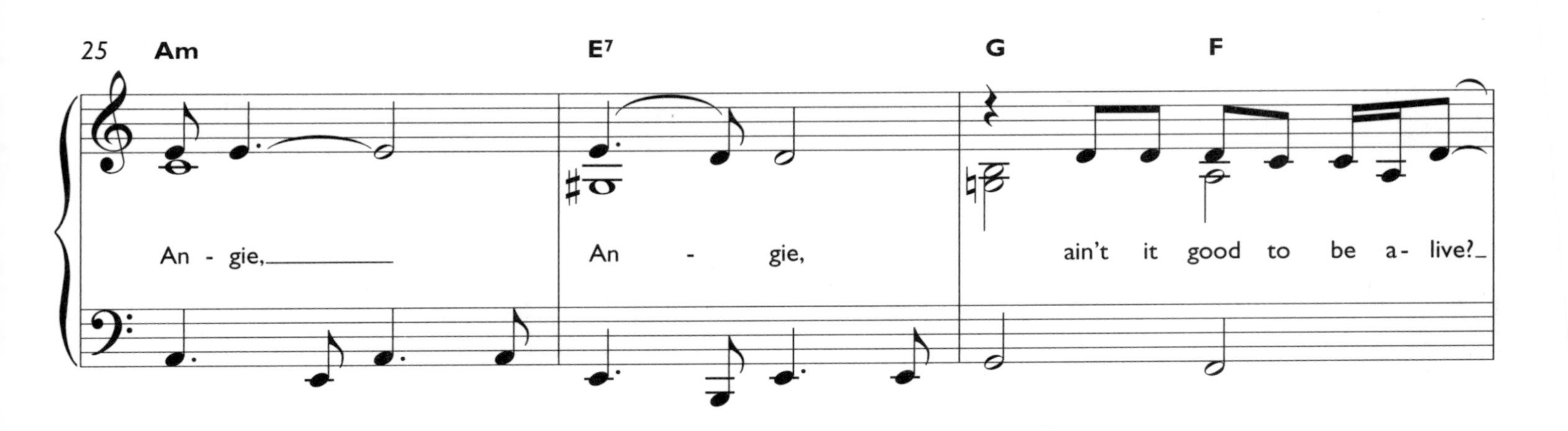
25
Am
E7
G
F
An - gie,
An - gie,
ain't it good to be a- live?

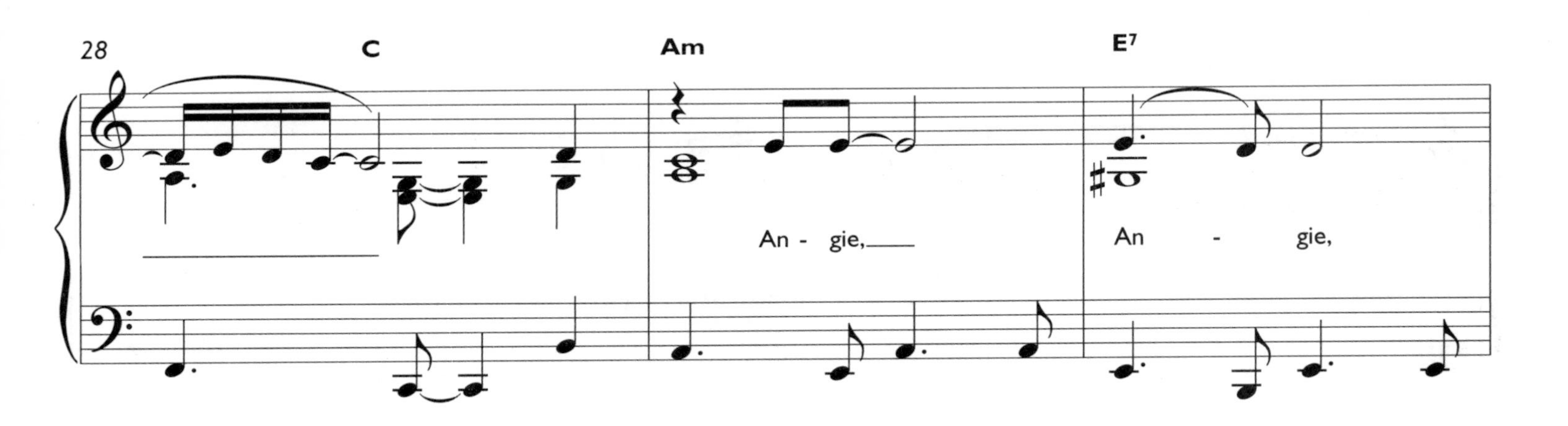
28
C
Am
E7
An - gie,
An - gie,

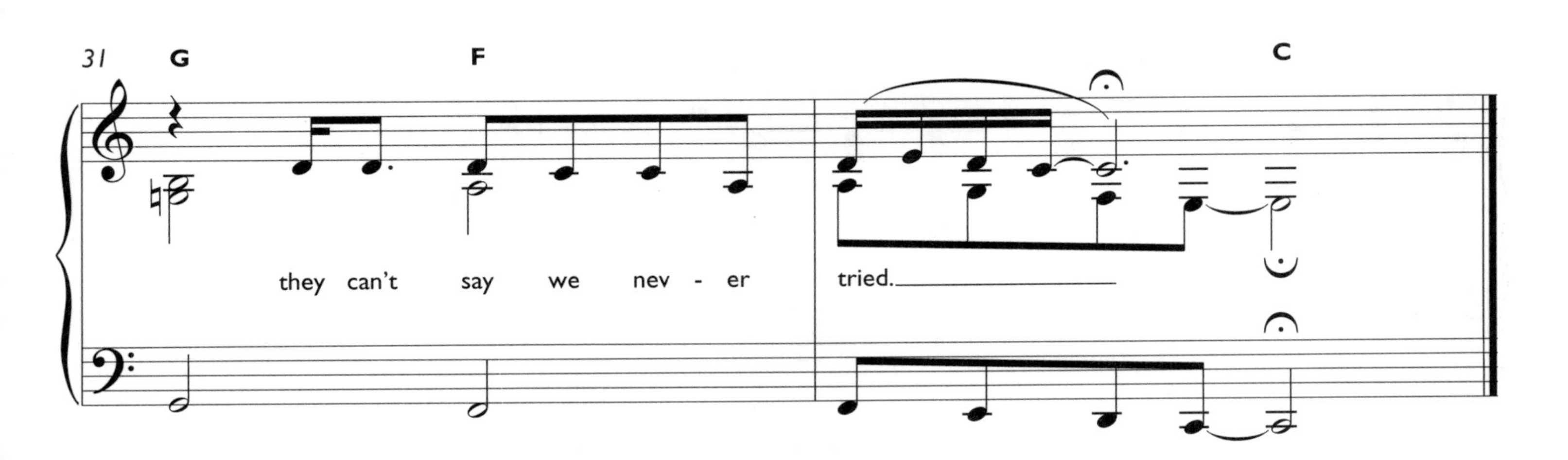
31
G
F
C
they can't say we nev - er
tried.

Angels

Words & Music by Robbie Williams & Guy Chambers

13
Dm7
B♭
E♭
un - fold.
So when I'm
ly - ing in my bed,
thoughts
mf

16
B♭/D
F
run - ning through my head,
and I
feel that love is dead,

18
E♭
B♭/D
F
C
I'm lov - ing an - gels in - stead.
And through it all,
she of - fers me pro - tec -
f

21
Dm
B♭
- tion, a lot of love and af - fec
- tion,
whe - ther I'm right or

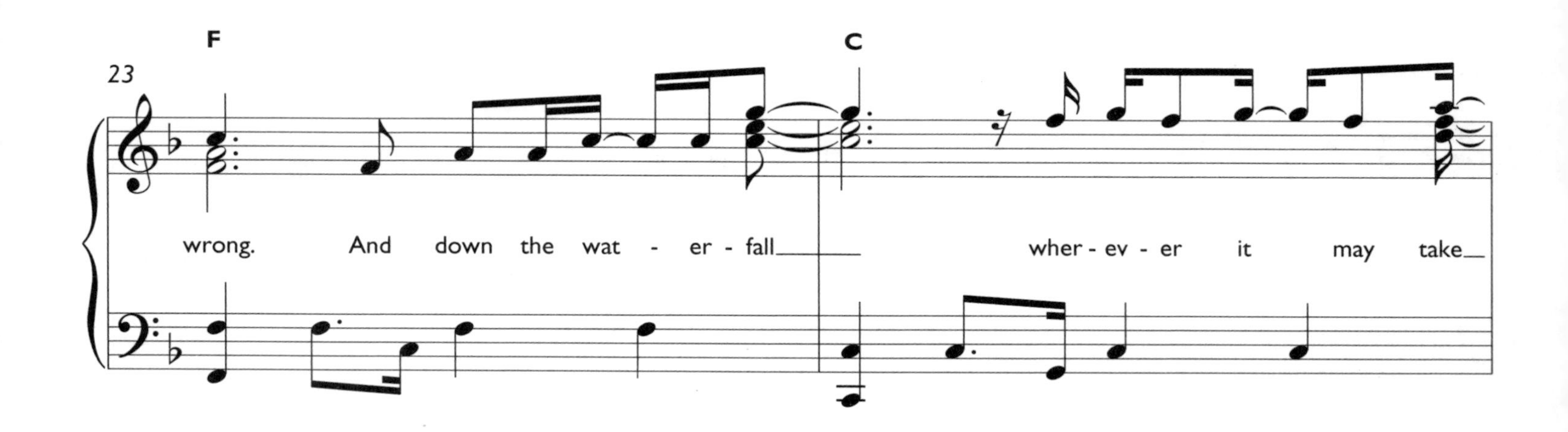
23
F
C
wrong. And down the wat - er - fall
wher - ev - er it may take

25
Dm
B♭
me, I know that life won't break
me, when I come to call,

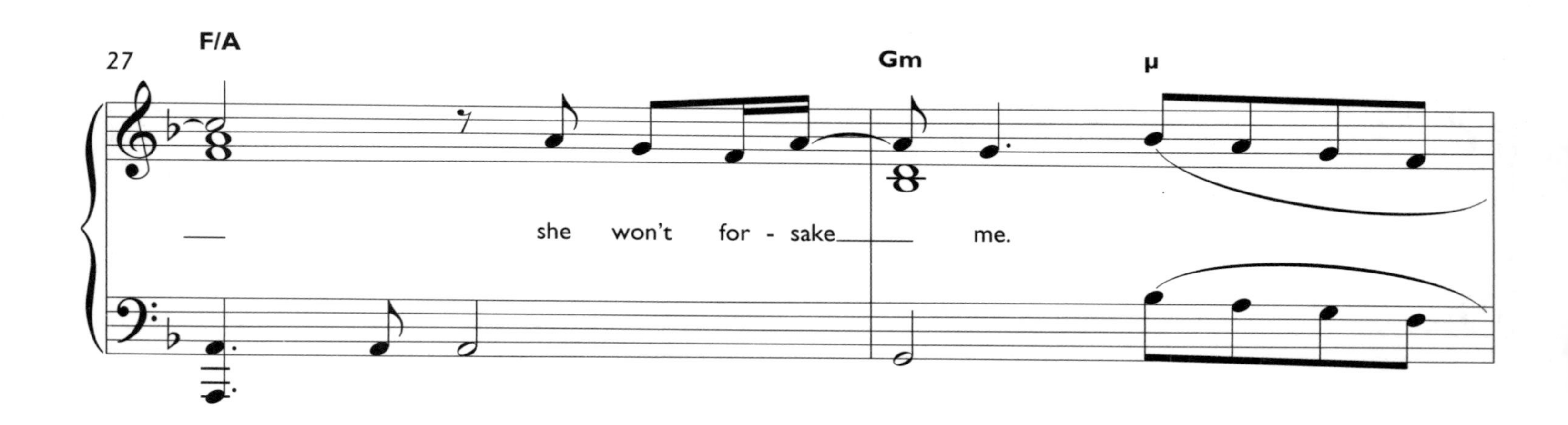
27
F/A
Gm
she won't for - sake
me.

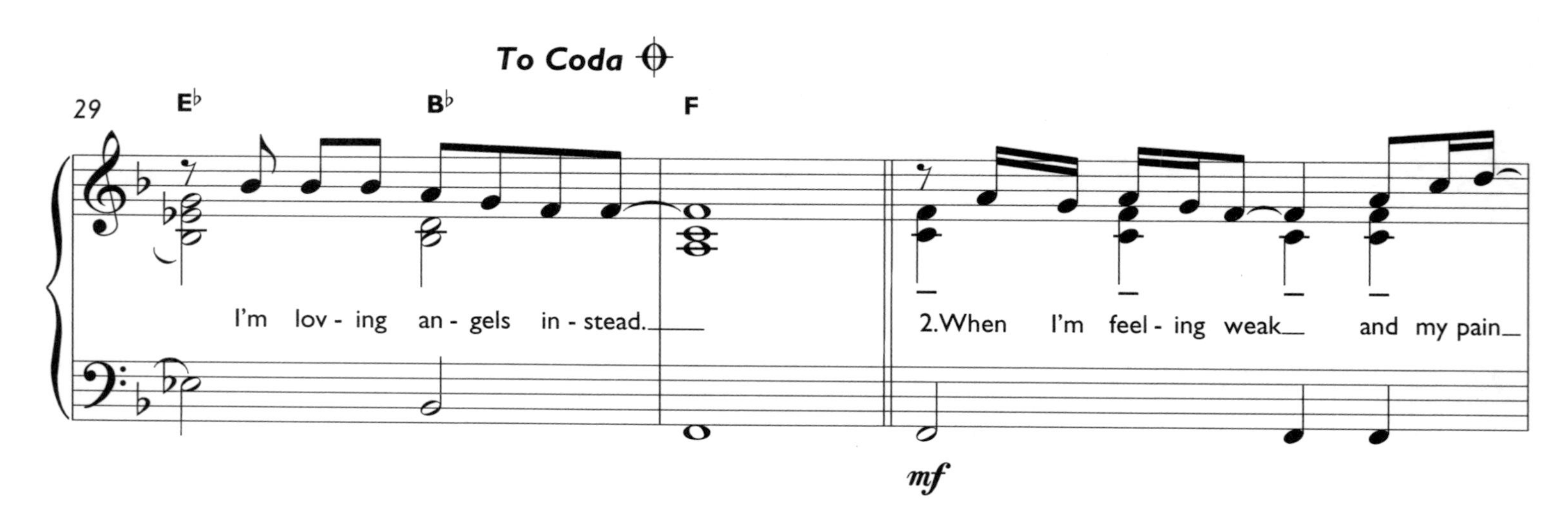
To Coda
29
E♭
B♭
F
I'm lov - ing an - gels in - stead.
2.When I'm feel - ing weak and my pain
mf

32
B♭
C
walks down a one - way street,
I look a - bove,

35
F
B♭
and I know I'll al - ways be blessed with love,

38
C
E♭
B♭/D
and as the feel - ing grows, she brings flesh to my bones and

D.S. al Coda
41
F
3
E♭
B♭/D
F
when love is dead, I'm lov - ing an - gels in - stead. And through it all,
f

Coda

44
F
Cm
Gm

47
F
Cm

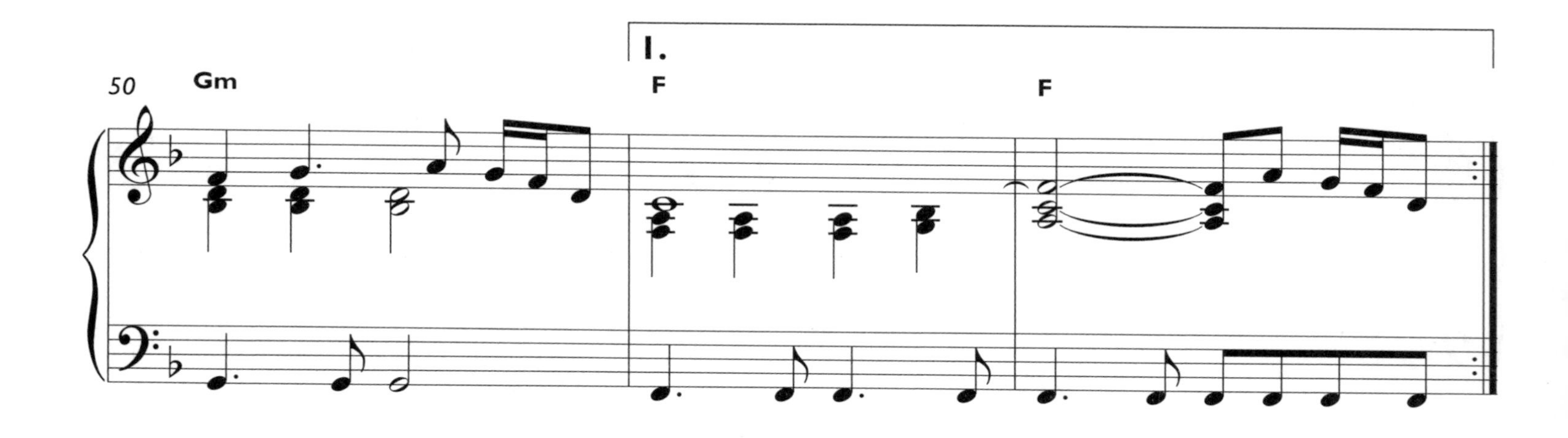

50
Gm
1.
F
F

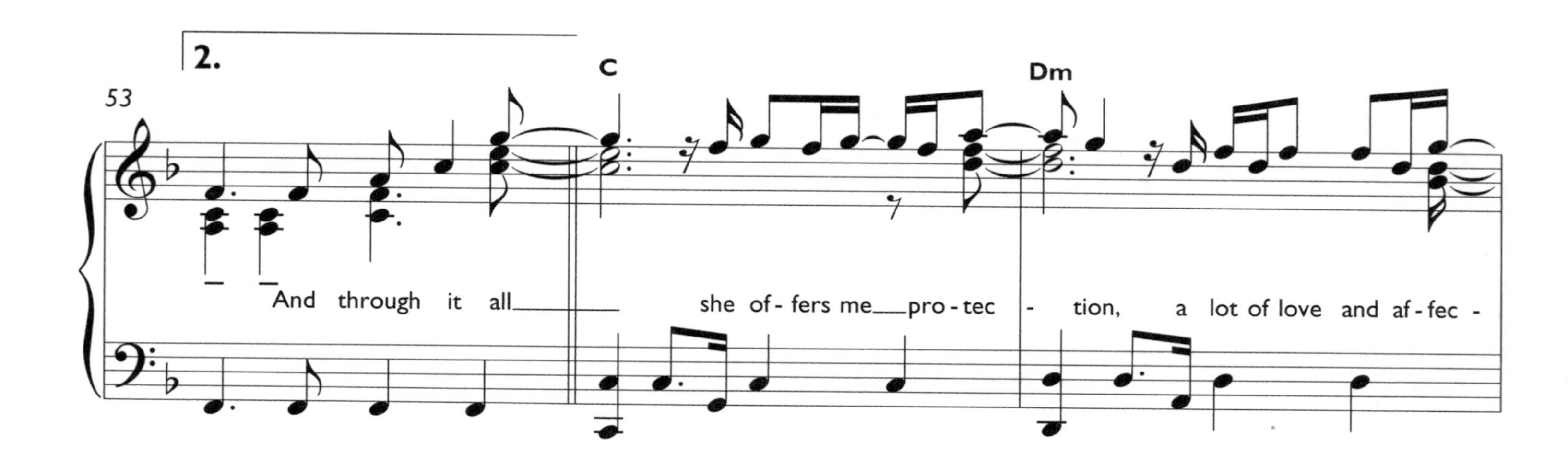

2.
53
C
Dm
And through it all she of-fers me pro-tec - tion, a lot of love and af-fec -

56
B♭
F
tion, whe - ther I'm right or wrong. And down the wat - er - fall
C
Dm
58
wher - ev - er it may take me, I know that life won't break
60
B♭
F/A
me, when I come to call, she won't for - sake
rit.
62
Gm
μ
E♭
E♭/B♭
F
me. I'm lov - ing an - gels in - stead.
p

Clocks

Words & Music by Guy Berryman, Chris Martin, Jon Buckland & Will Champion

13
E♭
B♭m
lights go out and I can't be saved, tides that I tried to
2. Con - fu - sion that nev - er stops, the clos - ing walls and
16
Fm
E♭
B♭m
swim a - gainst have brought me down up - on my knees,
tick - ing clocks: gon - na come back and take you home I
19
Fm
E♭
oh, I beg, I beg and plead, sing - ing: come out with
could not stop that you now know. Sing - ing: come out up
22
B♭m
Fm
things un - said; shoot an ap - ple off my head; and a
on the seas, curse missed op - por - tu - ni - ties. Am I

25
E♭
B♭m
trou - ble that can't be named: a ti - ger's wait - ing
a part of the cure, or am I part of
28
Fm
E♭
B♭m
to be tamed.
the dis - ease?
Sing - ing...
You
31
Fm
E♭
are.
You
34
B♭m
Fm
are.
37
E♭
B♭m
You
are.

Fm
E♭
B♭m
40
4 2 1
5 2 1
4 2 1
You
43
Fm
E♭
5 3 1
4 2 1
3 1
5 4 2
are.
3° & 4° You
B♭m
Fm
Play 4 times
46
5 4 2
5 4 1
are.
49
G♭maj7
And
no - - thing else
51
D♭
A♭6
com - pares,

53
G♭maj7
and no - - thing else
55
D♭
A♭6
com - pares,
57
G♭maj7
and no - - - thing else
D♭
A♭6
G♭maj7
59
com- pares,
62

65
E♭
B♭m
Fm
69
E♭
B♭m
3° & 4° You
are.
72
Fm
Play 4 times
E♭
B♭m
Home,
home,
where I
75
Fm
Play 4 times
E♭
want - ed to
go.
78
B♭m
Fm
Repeat to fade

Crazy

Words & Music by Thomas Callaway, Brian Burton, Gianfranco Reverberi & Gian Piero Reverberi

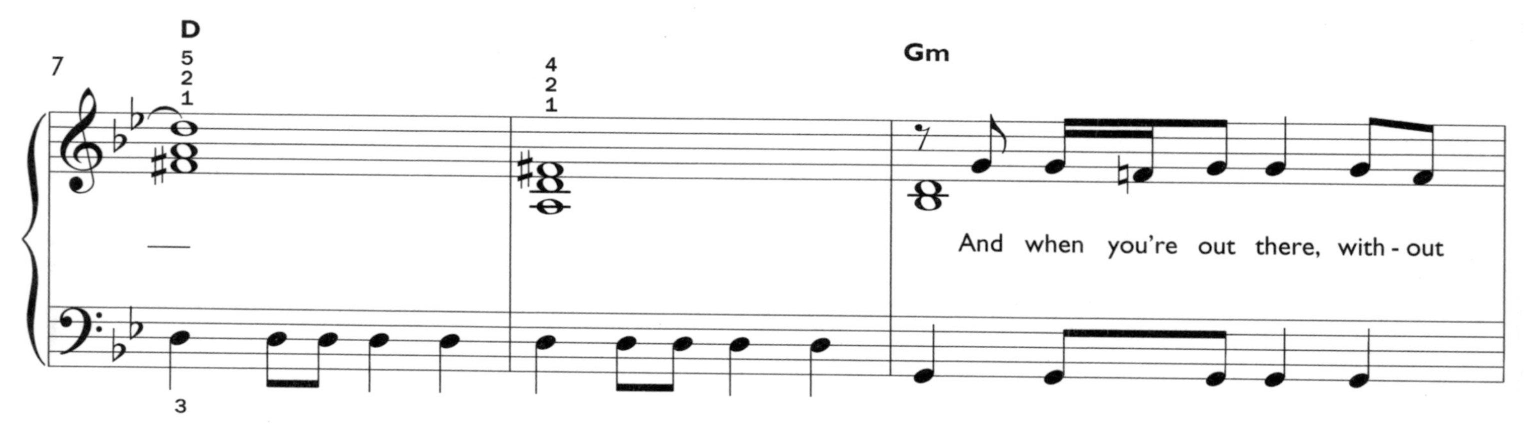

10
B♭
care, yeah, I was out of touch.__ But it
12
E♭
was - n't be - cause__ I did - n't know e - nough.____
14
D
I just knew too much.____
Does that make me cra-
17
Gm
B♭
- zy?____ Does that make me cra - zy?____ Does that make me cra-
21
E♭
D
- zy?____ Pos - sib - ly.________

Somebody Told Me

Words & Music by Brandon Flowers, Dave Keuning, Mark Stoermer & Ronnie Vannucci

13
Am
1. Break-ing my back just to know your name. Se-ven-teen tracks, and I've
2. Rea-dy, let's roll on-to some-thing new. Tak-ing it's toll and I'm
16
Dm
1° only
F
had it with this game.
leav-ing with-out you.

19
Am
Break-ing my back just to know your name, but hea-ven ain't close in a

22
place like this. A-ny-thing goes, but don't blink, you might miss.

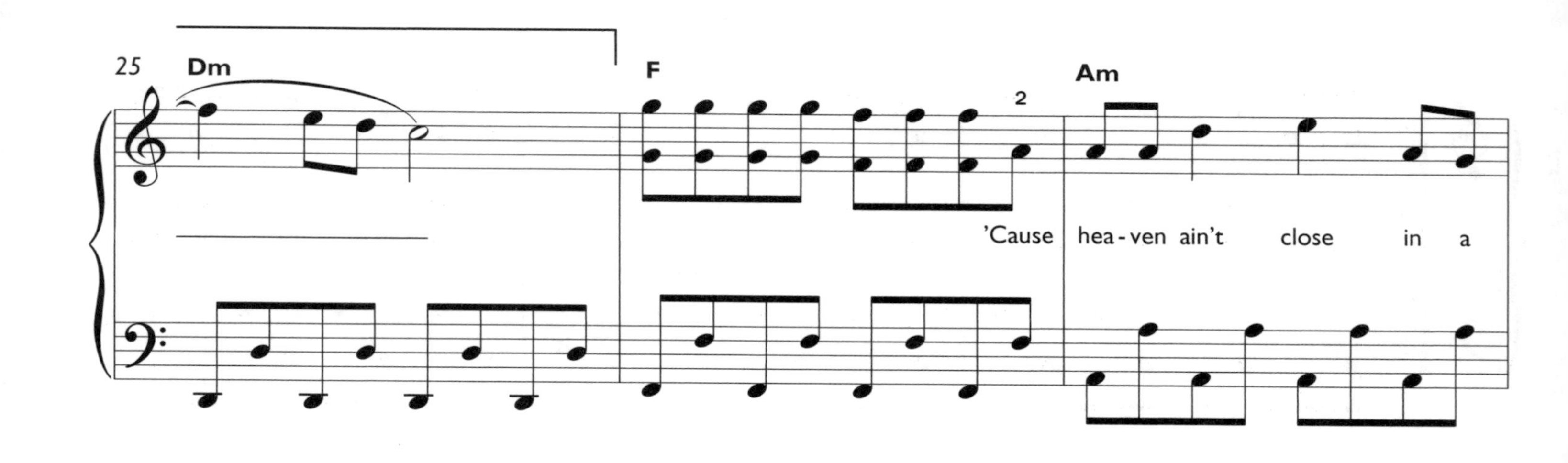
25
Dm
F
Am
'Cause hea-ven ain't close in a

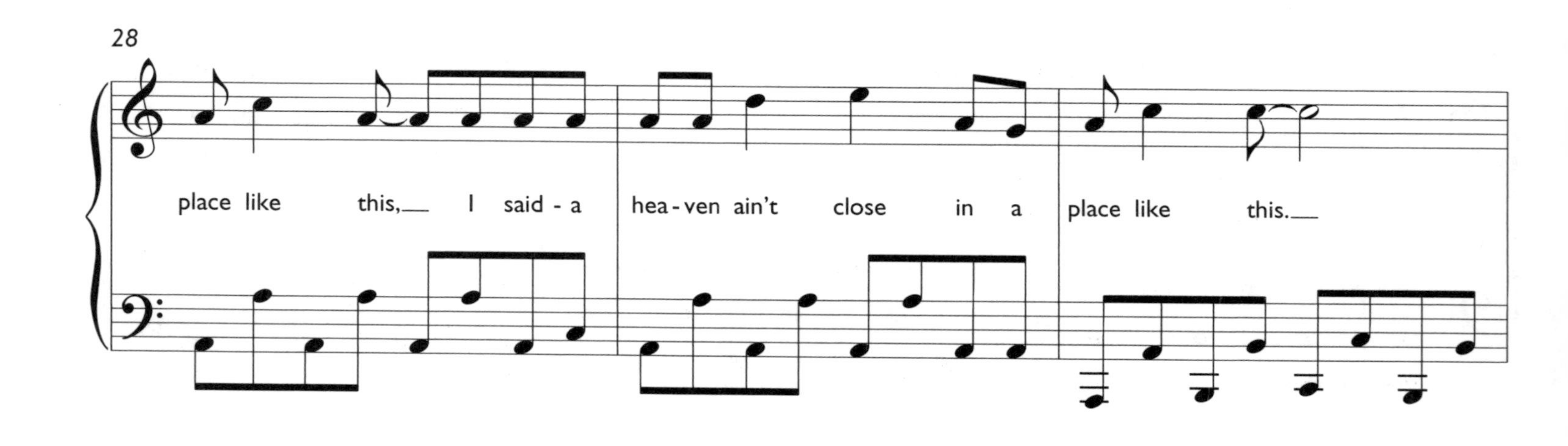
28
place like this, I said-a hea-ven ain't close in a place like this.

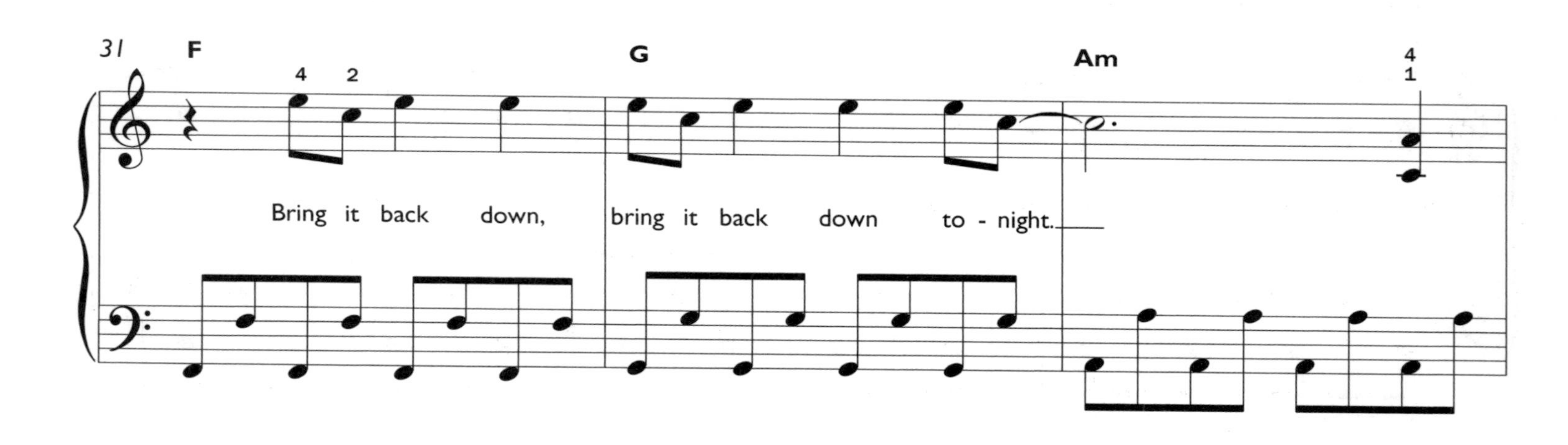
31
F
G
Am
Bring it back down, bring it back down to-night.

34
F
Nev-er thought I'd let a ru-mour ru-in my

G
N.C.
Am
37
moon - light.
Well, some - bo - dy told
me that you had a boy -
F
G
E
40
- friend who looked like a girl - friend that I had in Feb - ru - a - ry of last
Am
F
1.
43
year. It's not con - fi - den - tial. I've got po - ten - tial.
N.C.
2.
G
E
46
- tial, a rush - ing, a rush - ing a - round.

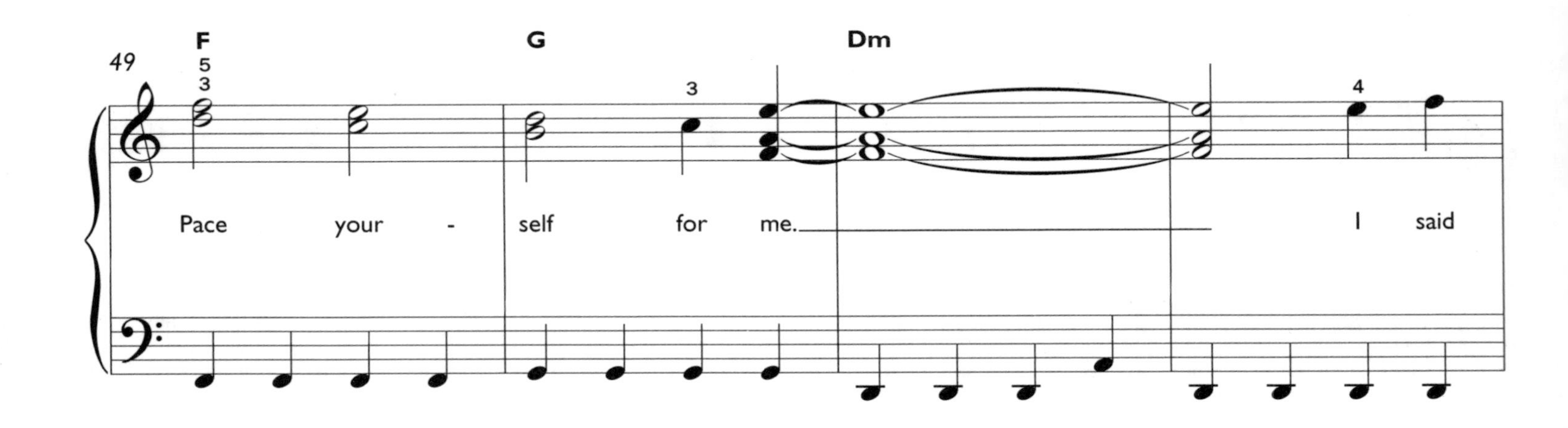
49
F
G
Dm
Pace your - self for me. I said

53
C
Dm
F
may - be ba - by, please. But I just don't

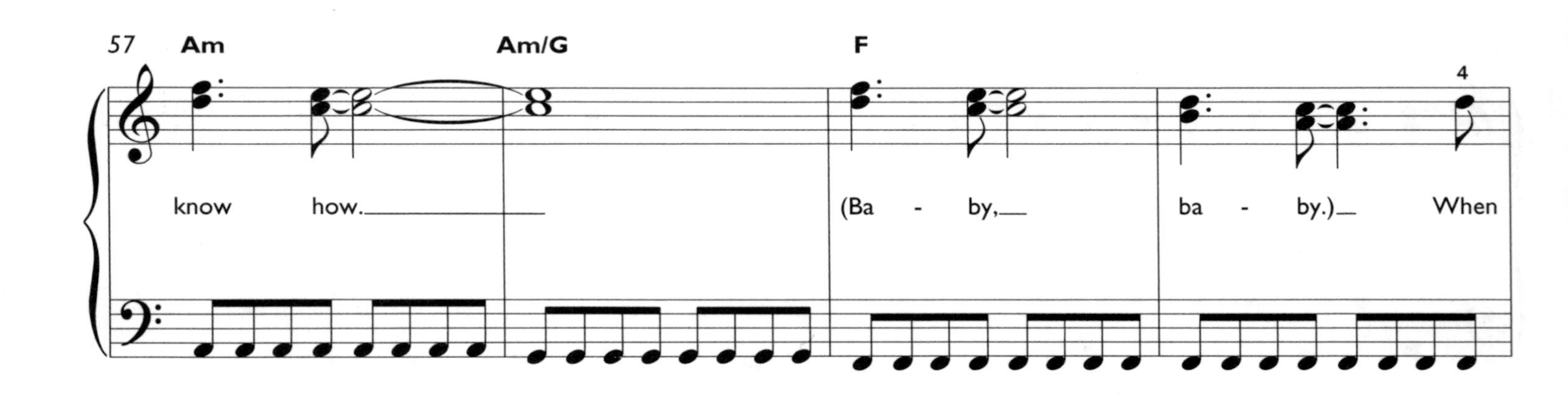
57
Am
Am/G
F
know how. (Ba - by, ba - by.) When

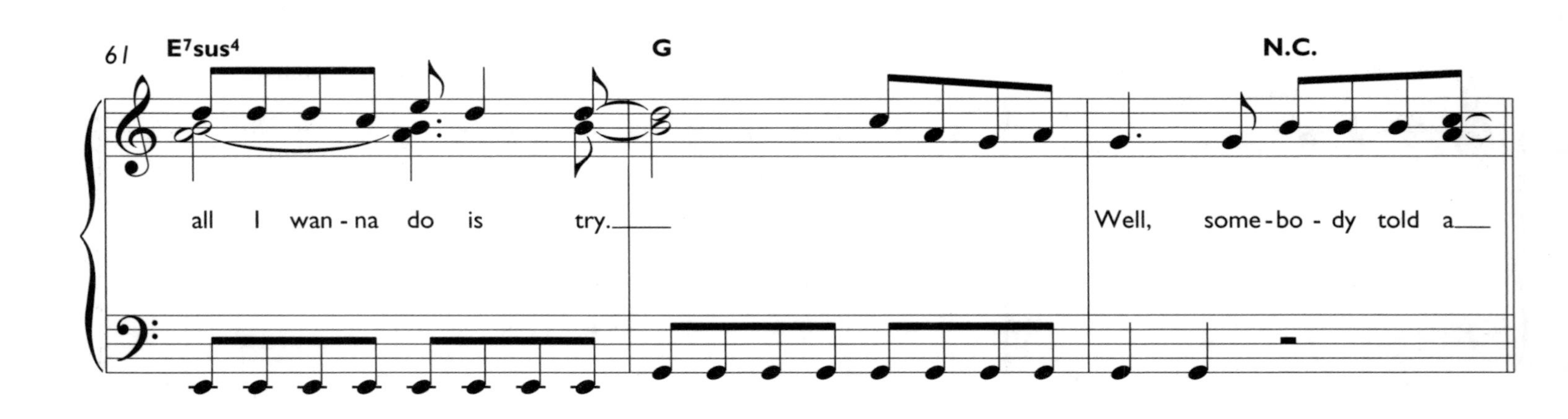
61
E7sus4
G
N.C.
all I wan - na do is try. Well, some - bo - dy told a

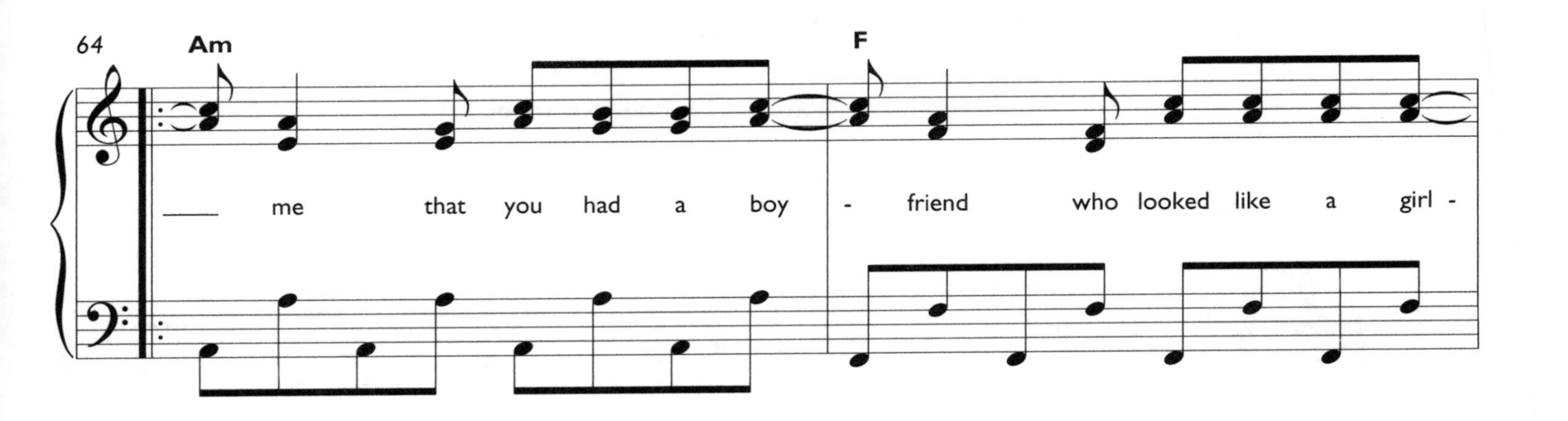
64
Am
F
me that you had a boy - friend who looked like a girl -

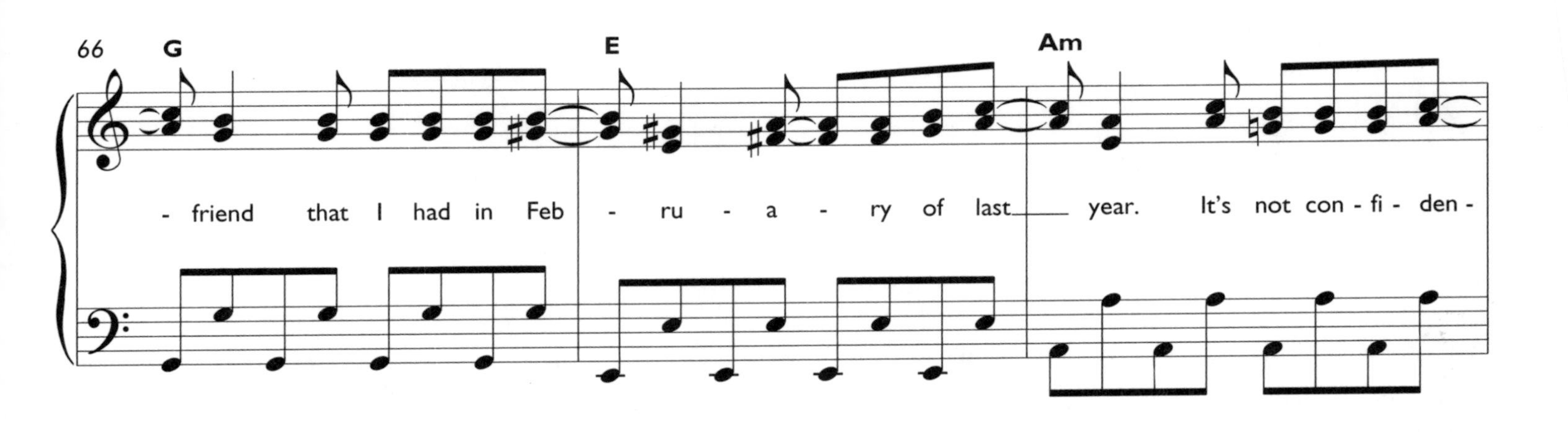
66
G
E
Am
- friend that I had in Feb - ru - a - ry of last year. It's not con - fi - den -

69
F
G
- tial. I've got po - ten - tial, a - rush - ing, a rush -

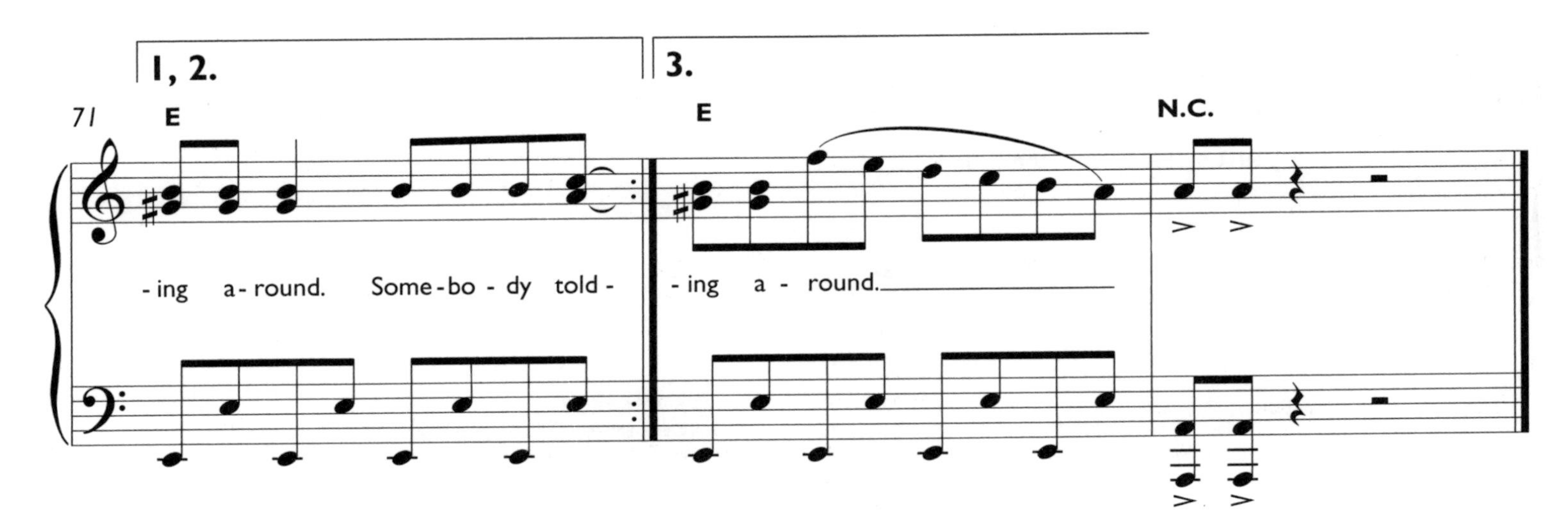
1, 2.
3.
71
E
E
N.C.
- ing a - round. Some - bo - dy told -
- ing a - round.

When You Say Nothing At All

Words & Music by Don Schlitz & Paul Overstreet

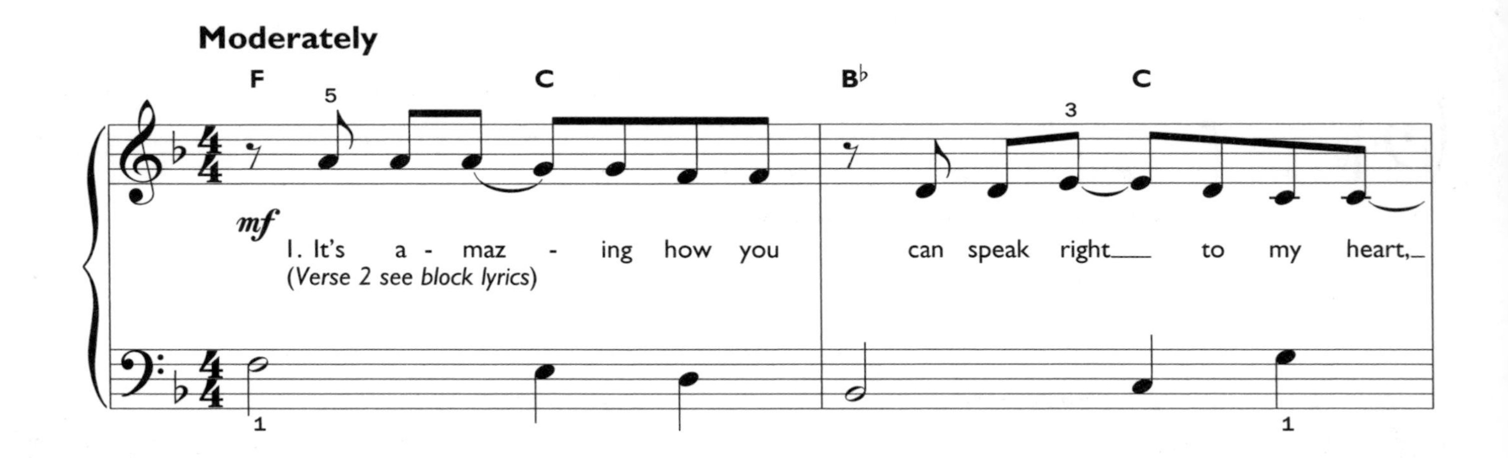

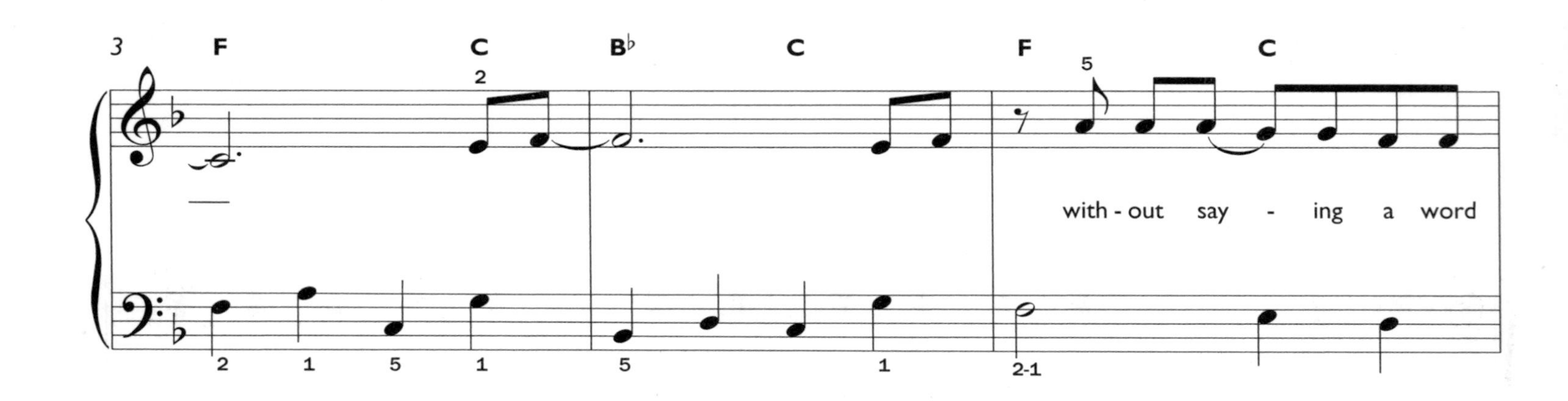

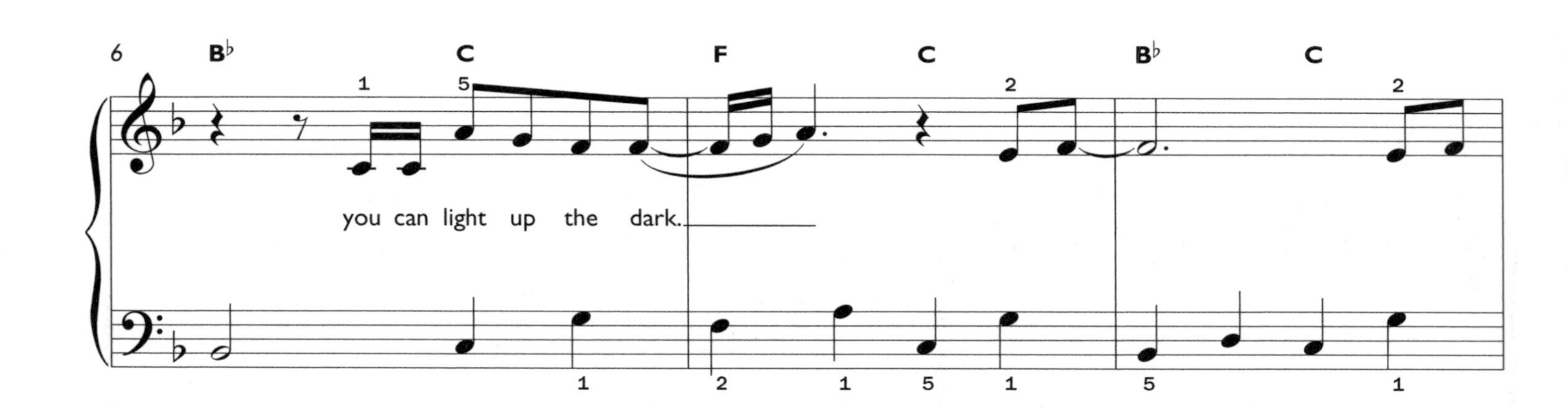

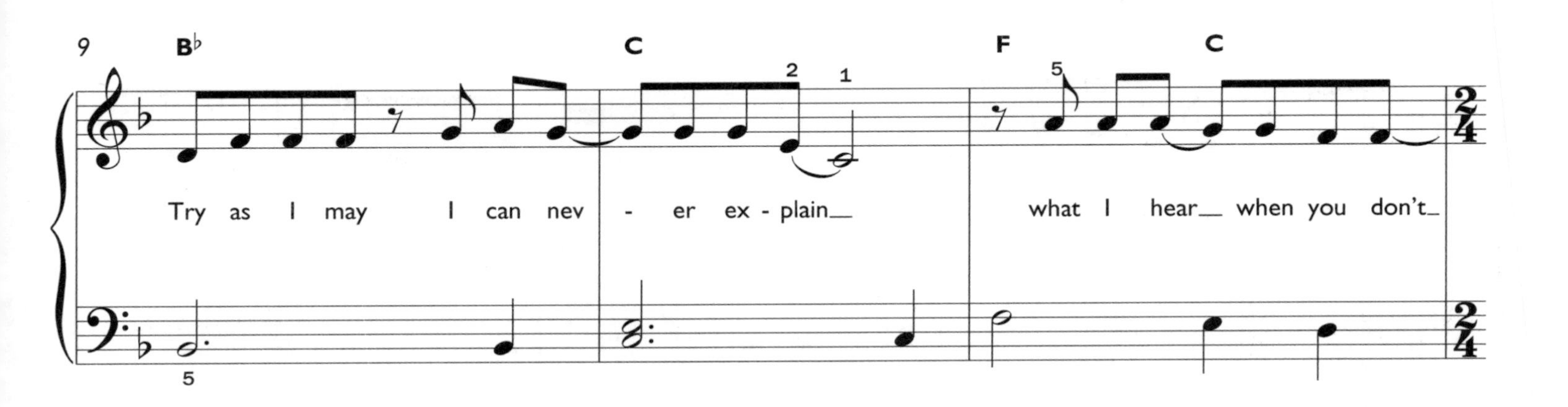
9
B♭
C
F
C
Try as I may I can nev - er ex - plain__ what I hear__ when you don't__

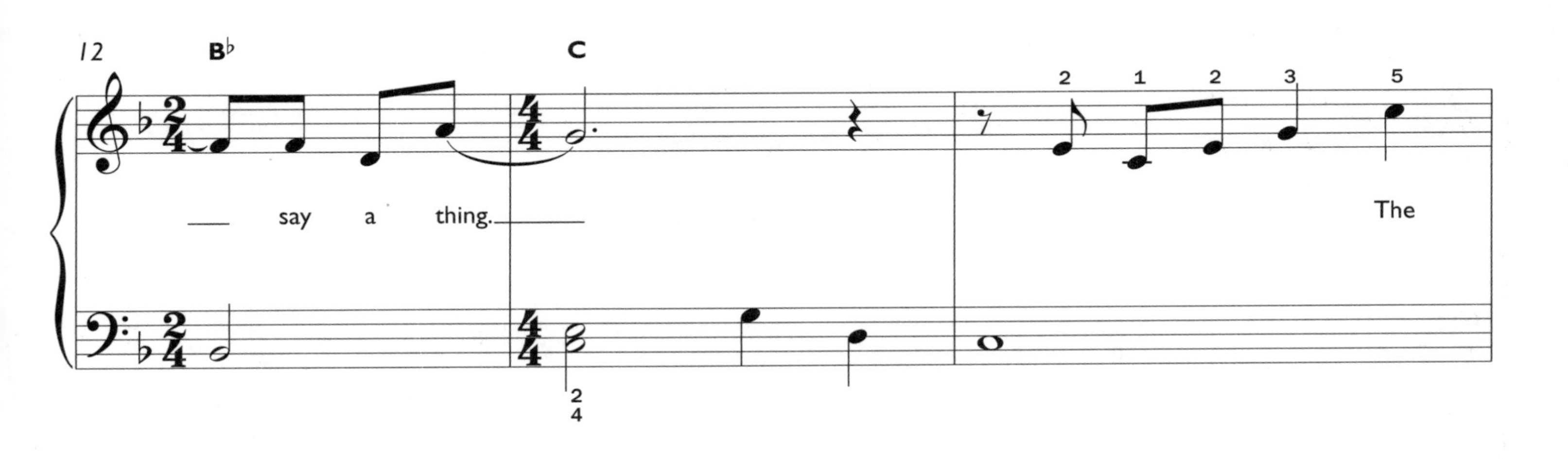
12
B♭
C
__ say a thing.____ The

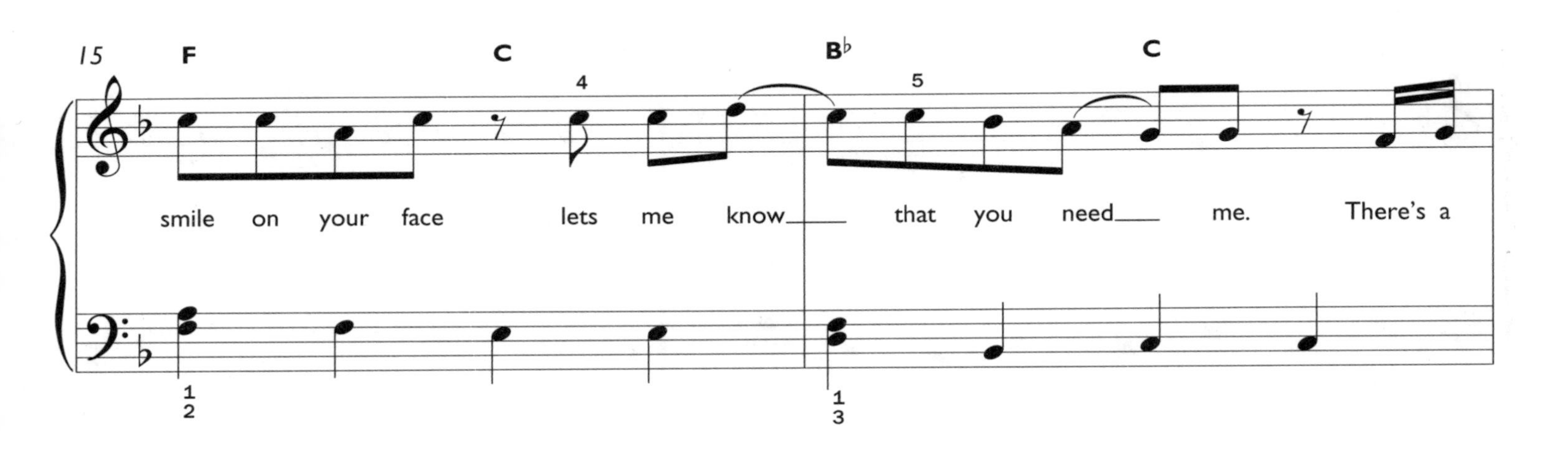
15
F
C
B♭
C
smile on your face lets me know__ that you need__ me. There's a

17
F
C
B♭
C
F
C
truth in your eyes say - ing you'll__ nev - er leave_ me. The touch of your hand says you'll catch__

20
B♭
C
B♭
C
3
1 2 4
1
me wher-ev-er I fall.
3
2
4

23
B♭5
1.
C
F
C
B♭
C
5
You say it best
when you say no-thing at all.
1

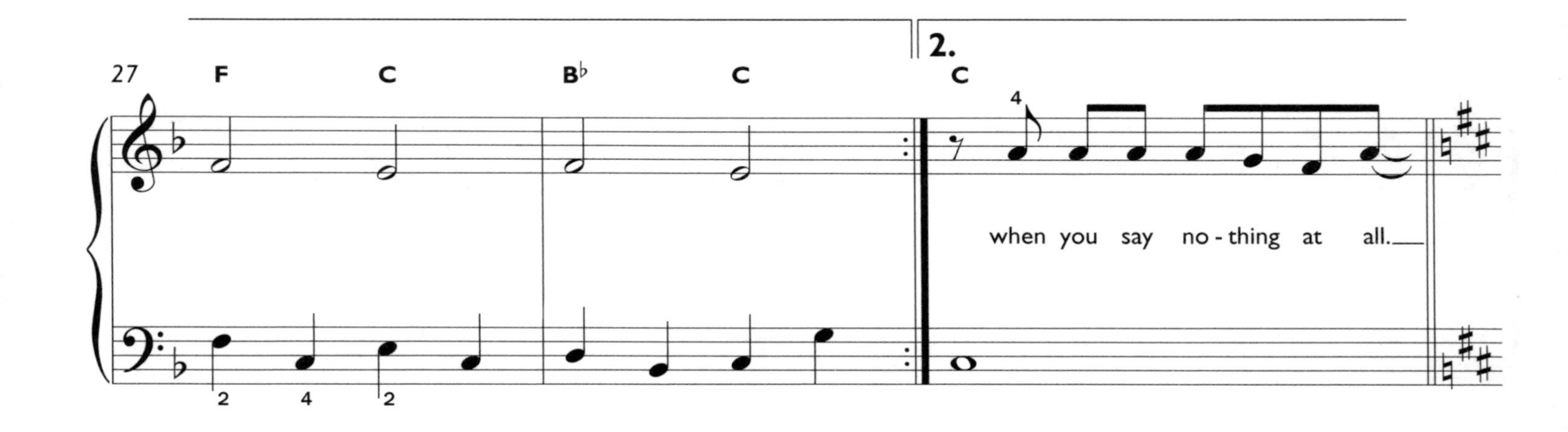
27
F
C
B♭
C
2.
C
4
when you say no-thing at all.
2 4 2

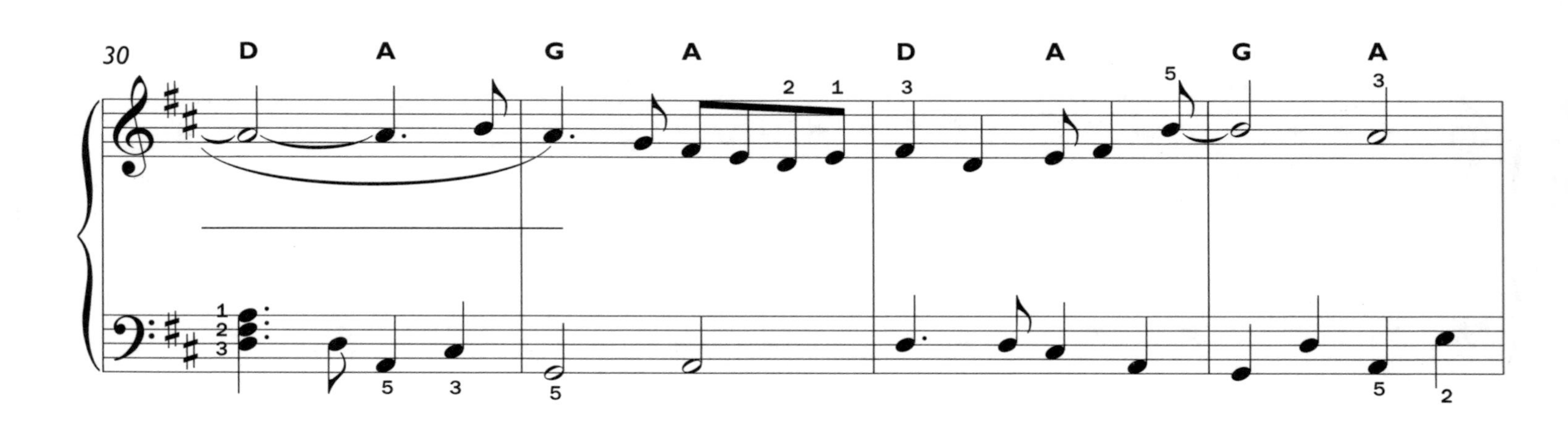
30
D
A
G
A
D
A
G
A
2 1
3
5
3
1
2
3
5 3
5
5
2

34
D A G A G A
The

38
F C B♭ C F C
smile on your face lets me know that you need me. There's a truth in your eyes say-ing you'll

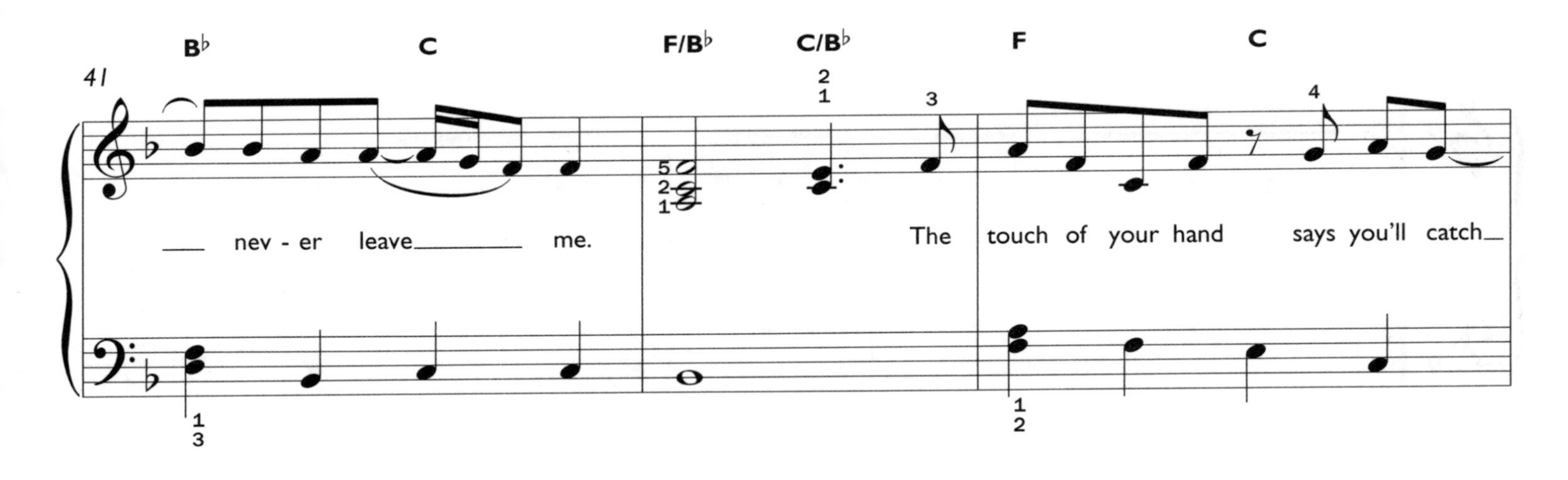
41
B♭ C F/B♭ C/B♭ F C
nev - er leave me. The touch of your hand says you'll catch

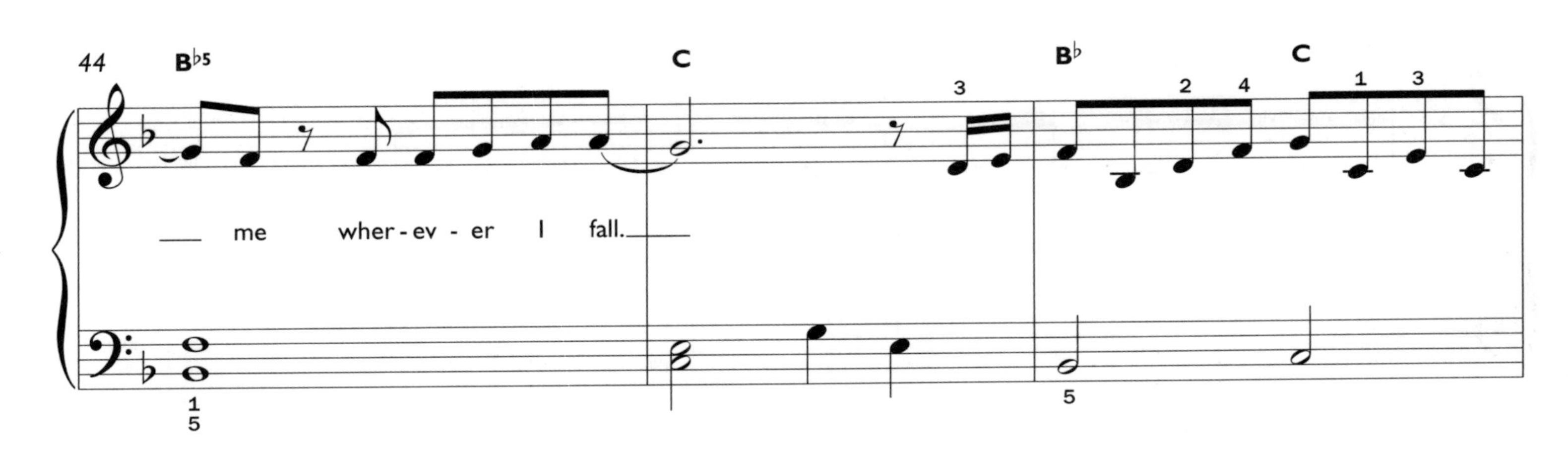
44
B♭5 C B♭ C
me wher - ev - er I fall.

47
B♭5
C
F
C
You__ say it best
when you say no - thing at all.____

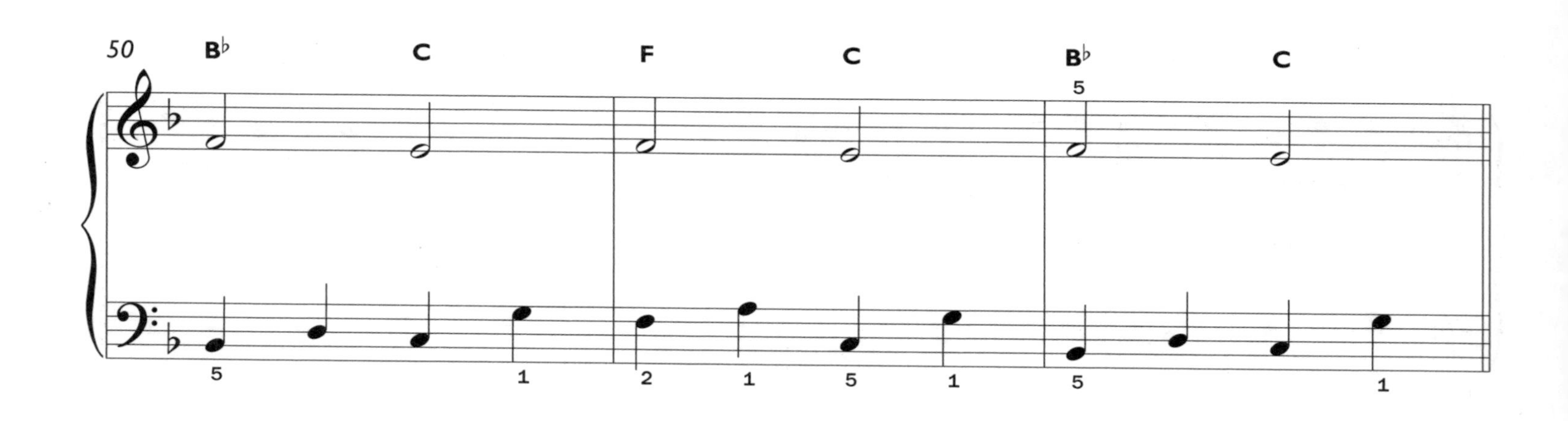
50
B♭
C
F
C
B♭
C

53
F
C
B♭
C
(You say it best____ when you say____
no - thing at all.)____

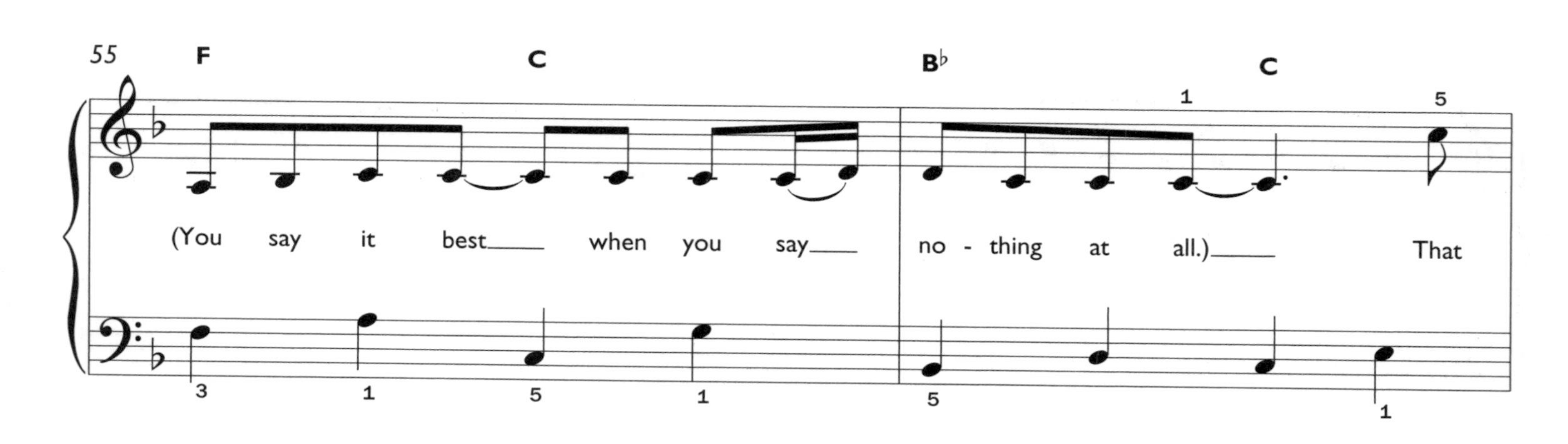
55
F
C
B♭
C
(You say it best____ when you say____
no - thing at all.)____ That

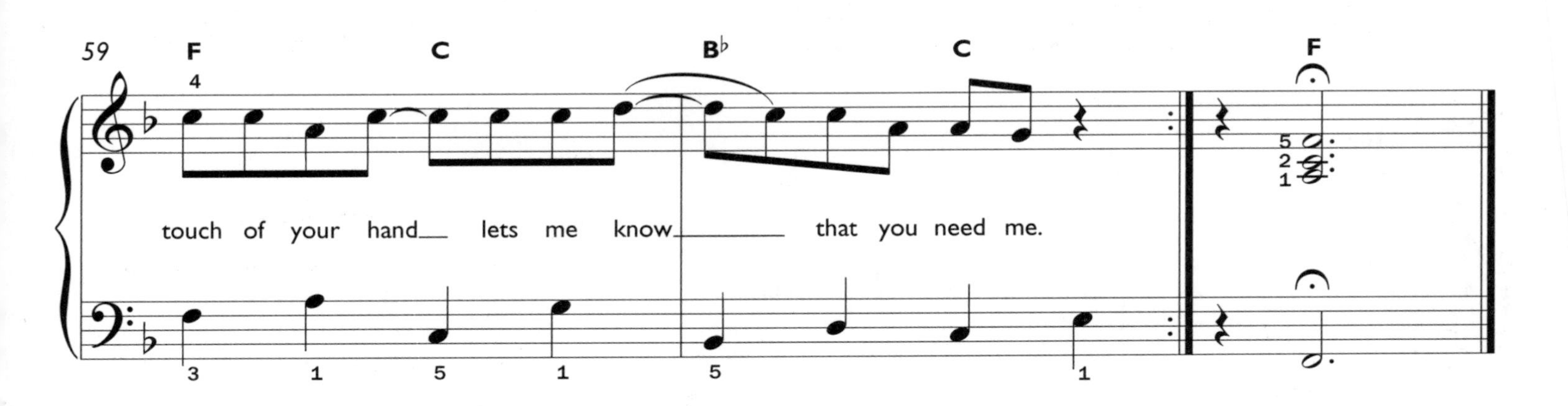

Verse 2:
All day long I can hear people talking out loud
But when you hold me you drown out the crowd
Try as they may they can never defy
What's been said between your heart and mine.

The smile on your face *etc.*

Creep

Words & Music by Thom Yorke, Jonny Greenwood,
Colin Greenwood, Ed O'Brien, Phil Selway, Albert Hammond & Mike Hazlewood

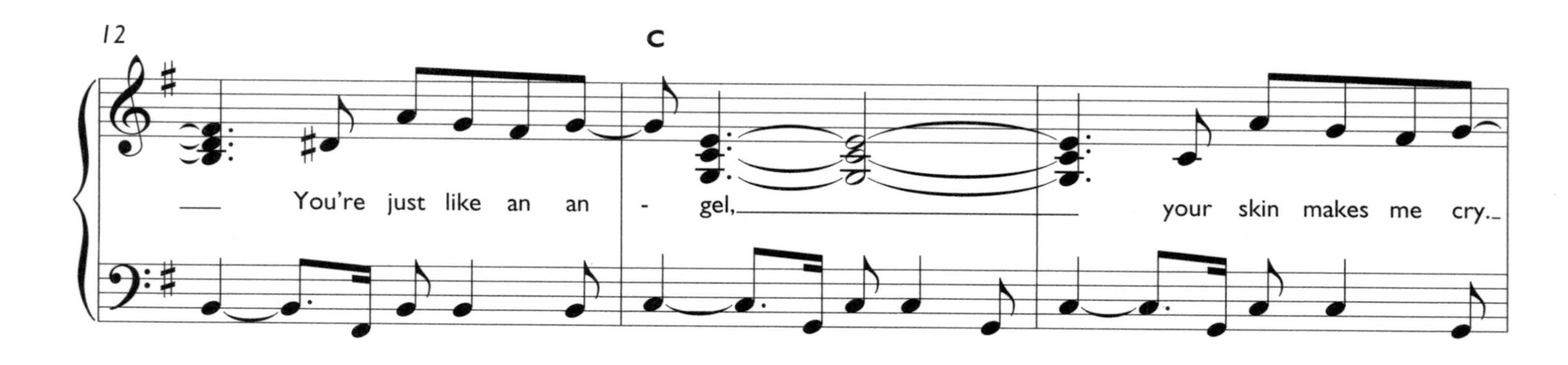

15
Cm
G
You float like a fea - ther
18
B
in a beau - ti - ful
world
I wish I was spe -
21
C
Cm
cial,
You're so fuck - in' spe - cial.
But I'm a creep
25
G
B
I'm a weird - o.
What the hell am I do - ing
29
C
Cm
here?
I don't be - long here.
What - ev - er makes you hap -

33
G
B
- py,
what - ev - er you
want.
36
C
You're so fuck - in' spe - cial.
I wish I was spe -
39
Cm
G
- cial
But I'm a creep,
42
B
C
I'm a weird - o.
What the hell am I do - ing here?
rit.
46
Cm
G
I don't be - long here.
I don't be - long here.

Life On Mars?

Words & Music by David Bowie

14
B♭/F
C7
Cm/E♭
seat with the clear - est view
and she's hooked to the sil - ver screen.
But the
18
Eaug
Fm
G♭
D♭
film is a sad - d'ning bore
for she's lived it ten times or more.
She could
22
Aaug
B♭m
D♭/B
spit in the eyes of fools
as they ask her to fo - cus on
25
B♭
E♭
Gm7
F♯aug
sail - ors fight - ing in the dance hall.
Oh, man!
Look at those cave - men
29
F
Fm
Cm7
E♭m7
go,
it's the freak - i - est show.
Take a look at the

33
B♭
E♭
Gm7
F♯aug
law - man
beat - ing up the wrong guy.
Oh, man!
Won - der if he'll ev - er know
37
F
Fm
Cm7
E♭m7
he's in the best sell - ing show.
Is there life on
41
Gm
F♯aug
B♭/F
Em7♭5
Mars?
45
F
F♯dim
Gm
Ddim
3
3
49
Am
B♭
B♭m
rit.
F

Have I Told You Lately

Words & Music by Van Morrison

Moderately slow ♩ = 88

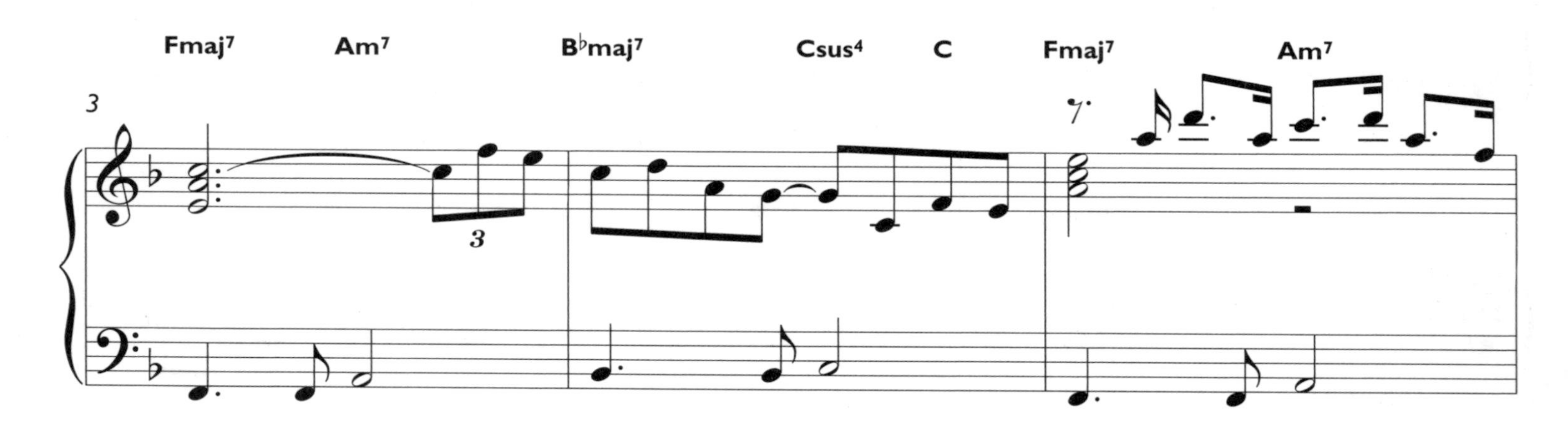

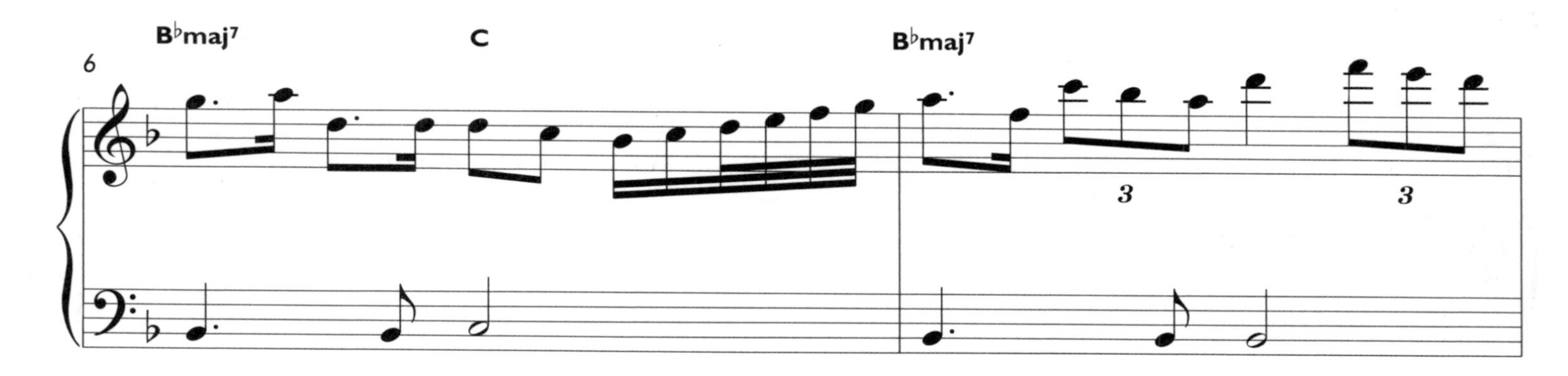

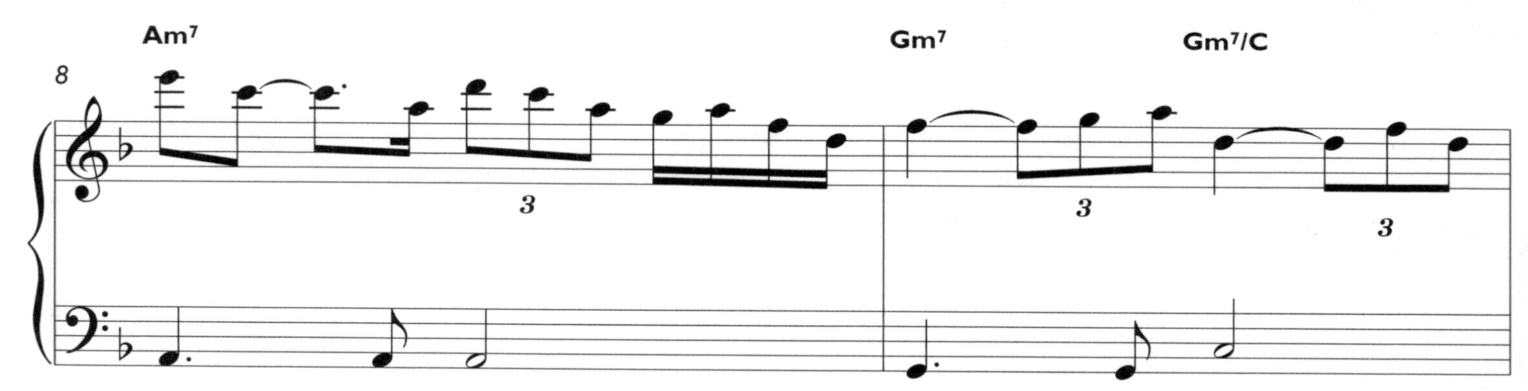

10
Fmaj7 B♭/C F Am7 B♭maj7 Csus4 C
1, 3, 5. Have I told you late - ly that I love___ you,___
(2.) morn - ing sun in all it's glo - ry___
4° Piano solo till *
13
F Am7 B♭ C
have I told you there's no - one___ a - bove___ you,___
greets the day with hope and com - fort too___
15
B♭maj7 Am7
fill my heart with glad - ness, take a - way my sad - ness,
and you fill my life with laugh - ter, you can make it bet - ter
17
Gm7 Gm7/C F B♭/C
1, 3.
ease my trou - bles that's what you do. 2. Oh the

2, 4.
F Gm7 Am7 B♭maj7
19
do.
* There's a love that's di - vine

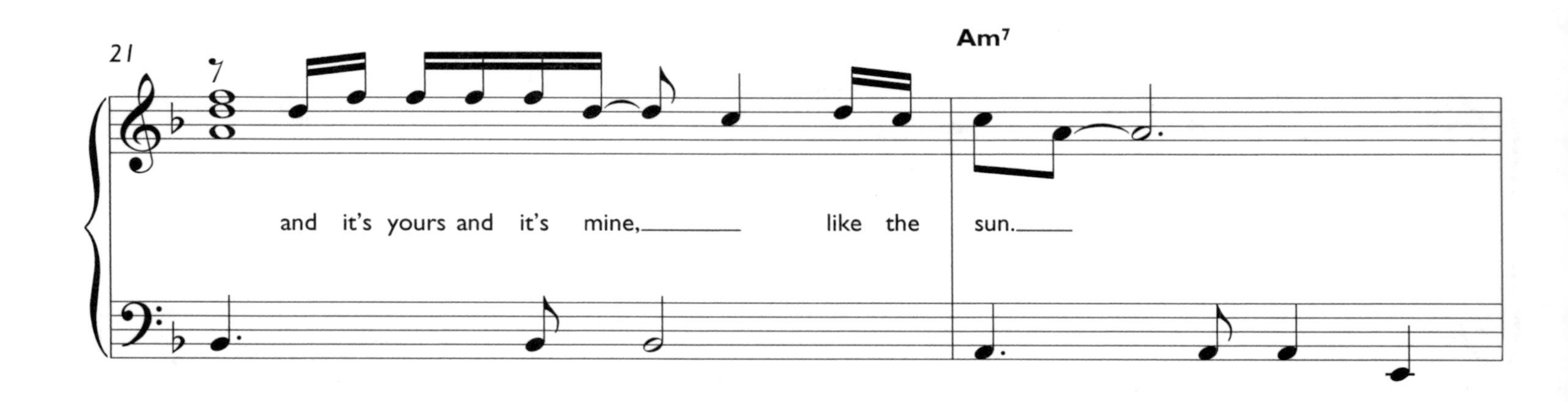
21
Am7
and it's yours and it's mine, like the sun.

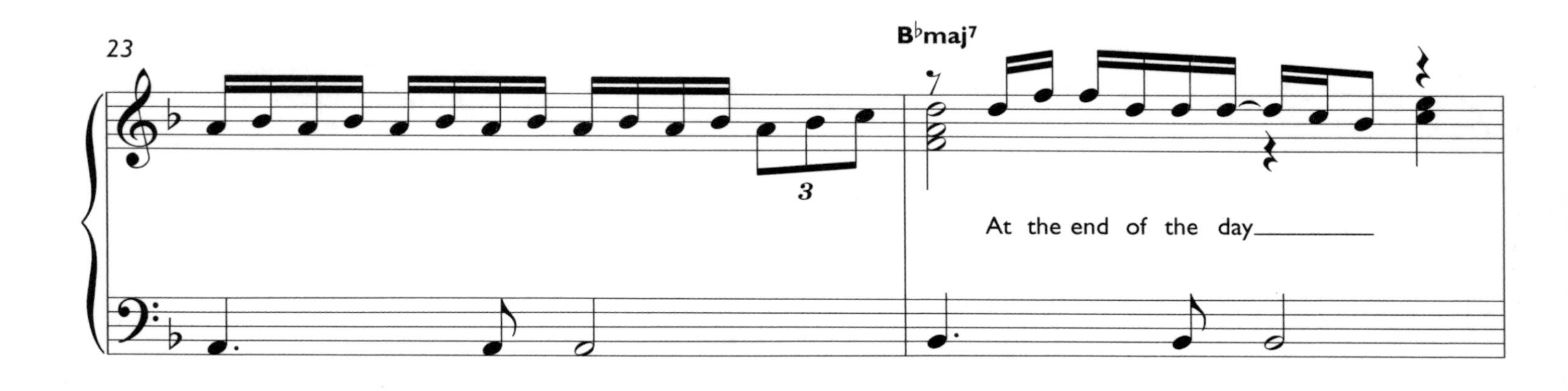
23
B♭maj7
3
At the end of the day

25
3
Am7
B♭/C
we should give thanks and pray to the one.
3, 5. Have I

5.
F
Gm7
Am7
B♭maj7
28
3
3
3
do.
Fill my heart with glad - ness,

Am7
Gm7
Gm7/C
30
3
3
take a - way my sad - ness,
ease my trou - bles that's what you

1.
2.
F
Gm7
Am7
F
32
3
3
3
do.
do.

Wild World

Words & Music by Cat Stevens

G Cmaj7 F Dm
care, hope you have a lot of nice things to wear;__ but then a lot of nice things turn
care, hope you make a lot of nice friends out there;__ but just re-mem-ber there's a lot of bad
E Dm6 G7 C
bad out there.
and be - ware.
Oh, ba - by, ba - by, it's a
F G F C
wild world. It's hard to get by just u-pon a smile.
F
Oh, ba - by, ba - by, it's a wild world.
1.
G F C D E
I'll al-ways re - mem - ber you like a child, girl.__

2.
C D E Am D7
to next strain
child, girl.
3.
C rall. Fine G Cmaj7 F Dm
child, girl.
E Am7 D9
Ba - by I love you, but if you want to leave, take good
G Cmaj7 F Dm
care, hope you make a lot of nice friends out there. But just re-mem-ber there's a lot of bad
E Dm6 C7
D.S. al Fine
and be - ware.

Any Dream Will Do

(from 'Joseph And The Amazing Technicolor® Dreamcoat')

Music by Andrew Lloyd Webber

Lyrics by Tim Rice

Moderately bright

G⁷sus⁴ | G | C

mf

I closed my eyes,

4 G | C | F | C

drew back the cur - tain, to see for cer - tain

8 G | C | G | C

what I thought I knew. And in the East

12 G | C | F | C

the dawn was break - ing, and the world was wak - ing

16 G C C7 F F6
an - y dream will do. f A crash of drums, a
20 Fmaj7 F6 D7 D9 C Da C
flash of light, my gol - den cloak flew out of sight, the col - ours fad - ed
24 F C Dm7 C G Am7 G C G7 Gsus4
in - to dark - ness, I was left a - lone. Ah,
28 G C G C
mf may I re - turn to the be - gin - ning,
32 F C G C
the light is dim - ming and the dream is too.

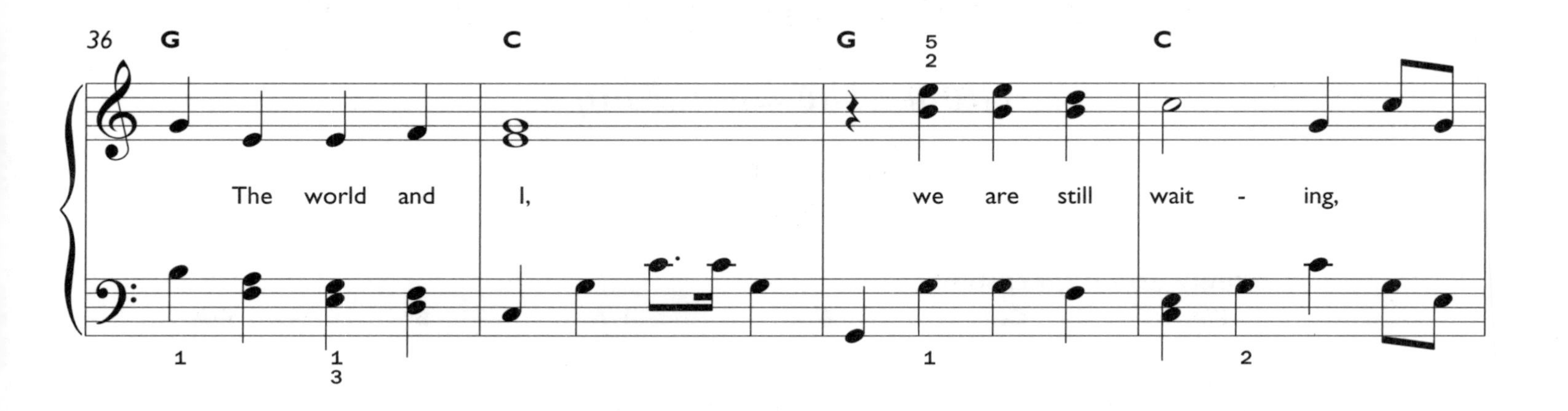
36
G C G C
The world and I, we are still wait - ing,

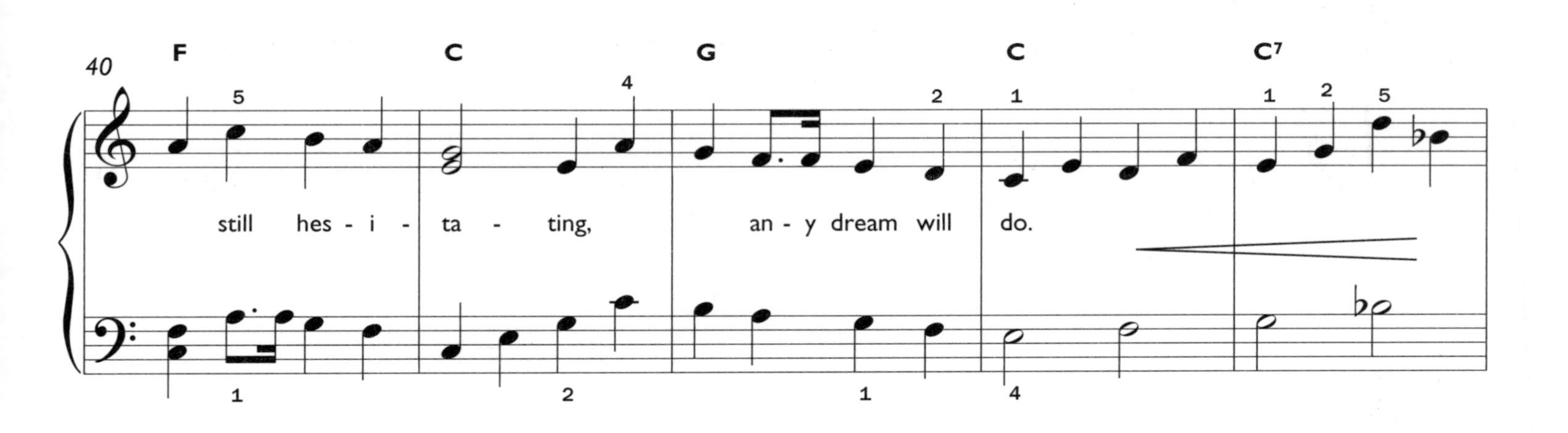
40
F C G C C7
still hes - i - ta - ting, an - y dream will do.

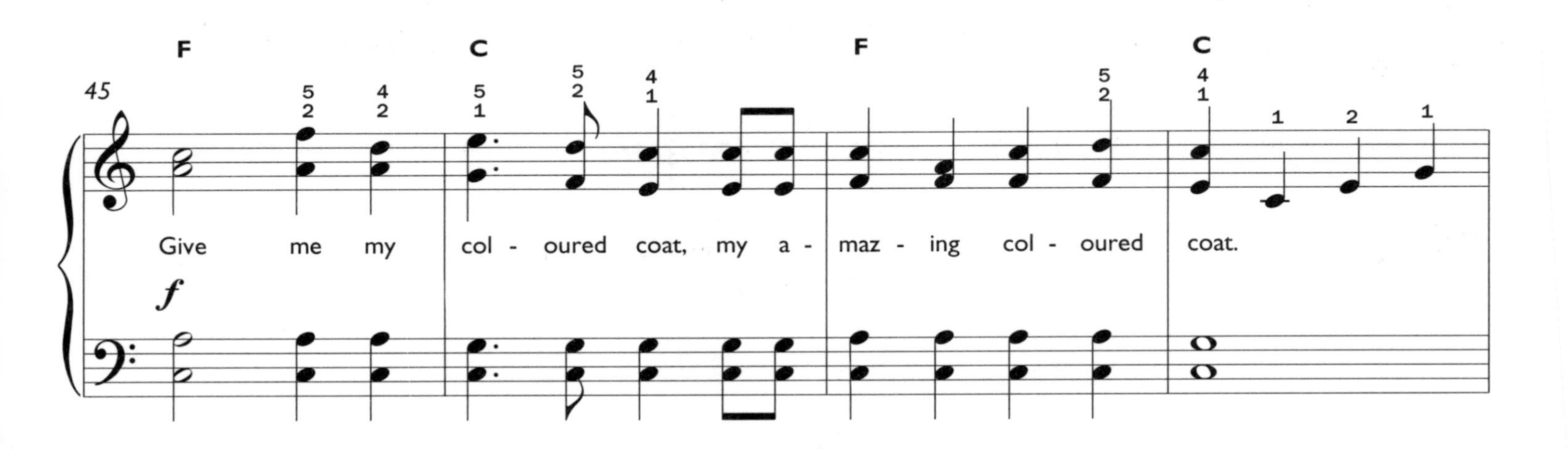
45
F C F C
Give me my col - oured coat, my a - maz - ing col - oured coat.
f

49
F C F C
Give me my col - oured coat, my a - maz - ing col - oured coat.

Can You Feel The Love Tonight?

(from 'The Lion King')

Words by Tim Rice
Music by Elton John

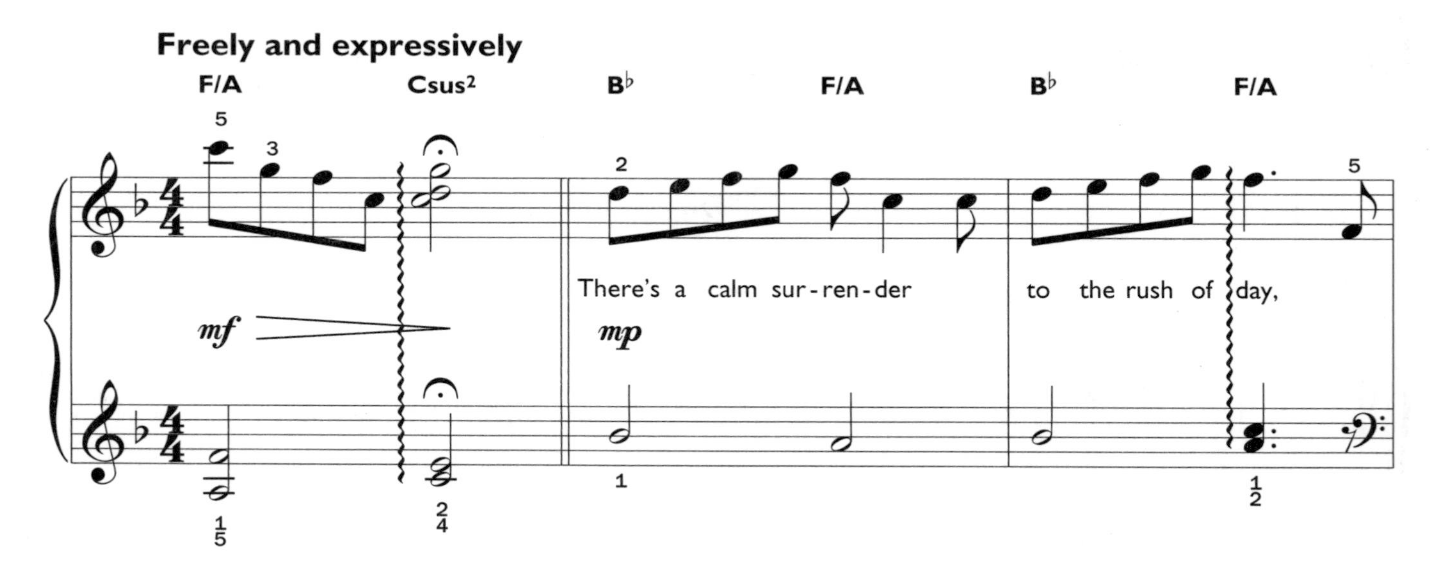

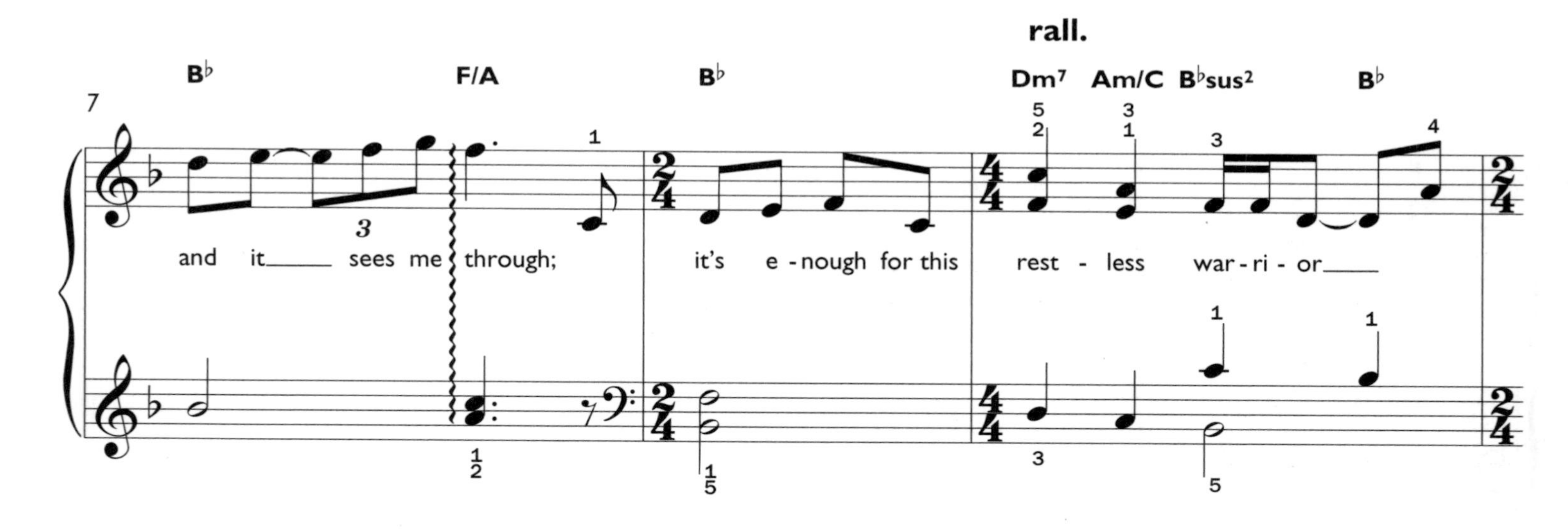

10
E♭
Csus2
just to be with you.
And
Moderately slow
F
C/E
Dm
B♭
13
can you feel the love to - night?
mf
F/A
B♭
Csus4
C
15
It is where we are.
B♭
F
Dm7
Am/C
B♭
B♭/A
17
It's e - nough for this wide - eyed wand - er - er

Gm F/A Gm/B♭ B♭maj7 C
that we got this far.
mp
B♭ F B♭ F/A F
There's a time for ev-'ry-one,
if they on-ly learn
B♭ F Gm7 Csus4
that the twist-ing kal-eid-o-scope
moves us all in turn.
B♭ F B♭ F
There's a rhyme and rea-son
to the wild out-doors,

B♭ F/A E♭
when the heart of this star-crossed voy - ag - er beats in time with
C7 F C/E Dm
yours. Can you feel the love
B♭
to - night?
F F/A B♭ F/B♭
It is where we
C B♭ F
are. It's e - nough for this

Dm7 Am/C B♭ Gm F/A Gm/B♭ Dm C
wide - eyed wand - er - er that we got this far.
G D Em
Can you feel the love
f
C G G/B C G/C
to - night, how it's laid to
D C G G/F♯
rest? It's e - nough to make
mf

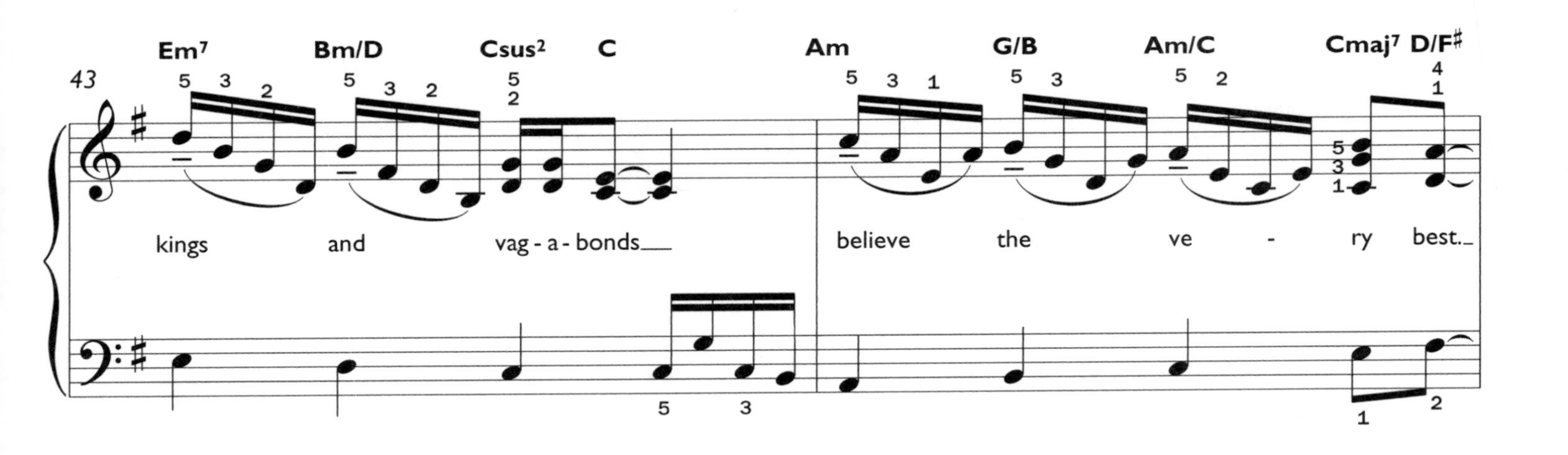
Em7 Bm/D Csus2 C Am G/B Am/C Cmaj7 D/F#
kings and vag - a - bonds
believe the ve - ry best.

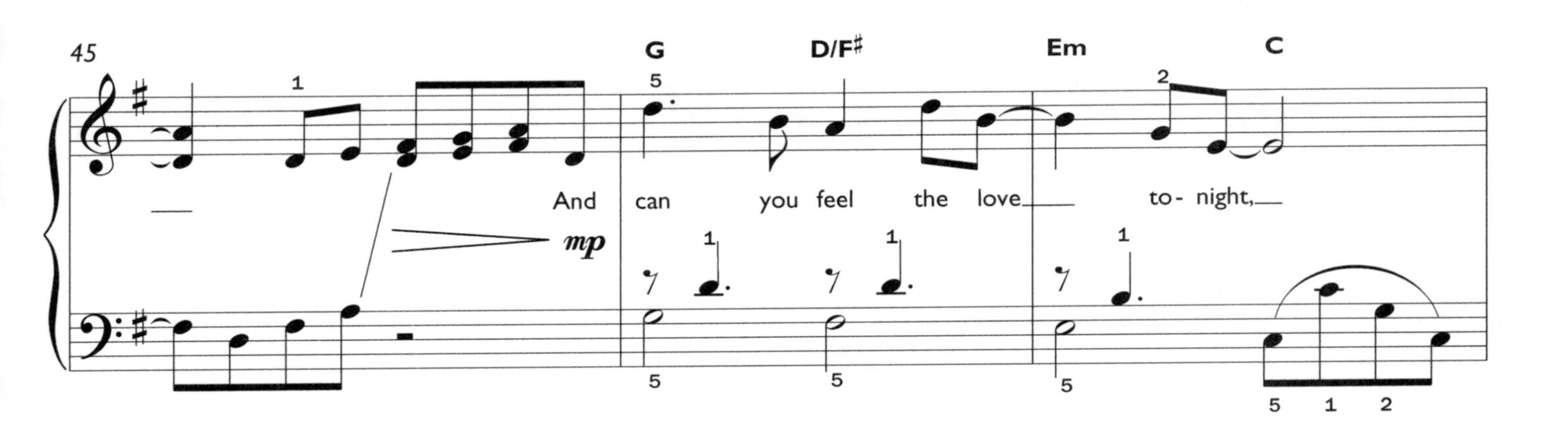
G D/F# Em C
And can you feel the love to - night,

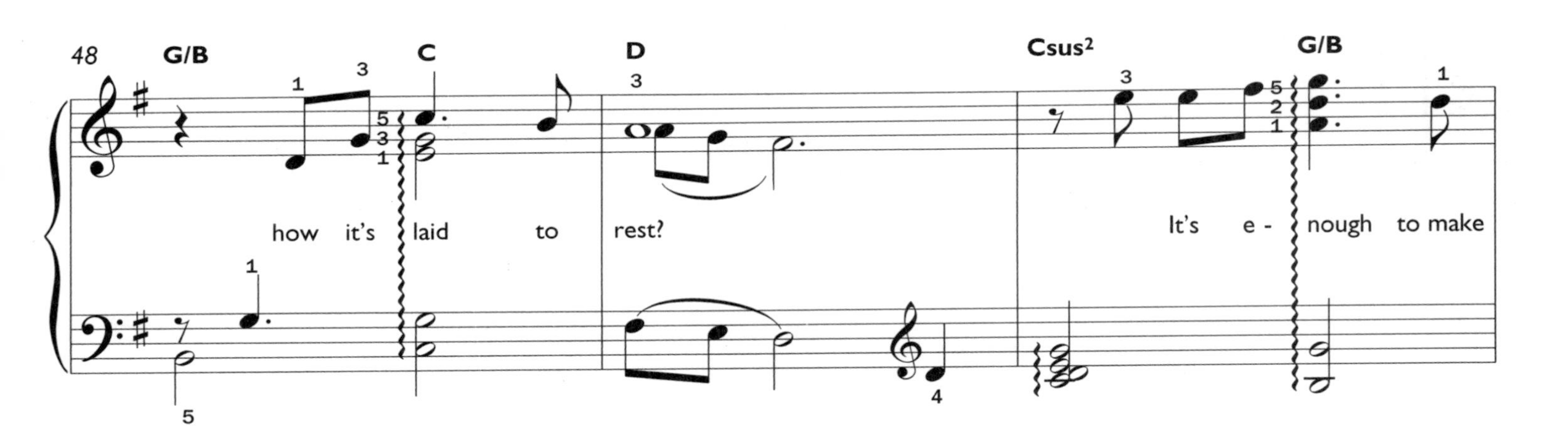
G/B C D Csus2 G/B
how it's laid to rest?
It's e - nough to make

rall.
molto rit.
Em7 Bm/D Csus2 Am G/B Dsus4 D C G
kings and vaga - bonds be - lieve the ve - ry best.

Consider Yourself

(from 'Oliver!')

Words & Music by Lionel Bart

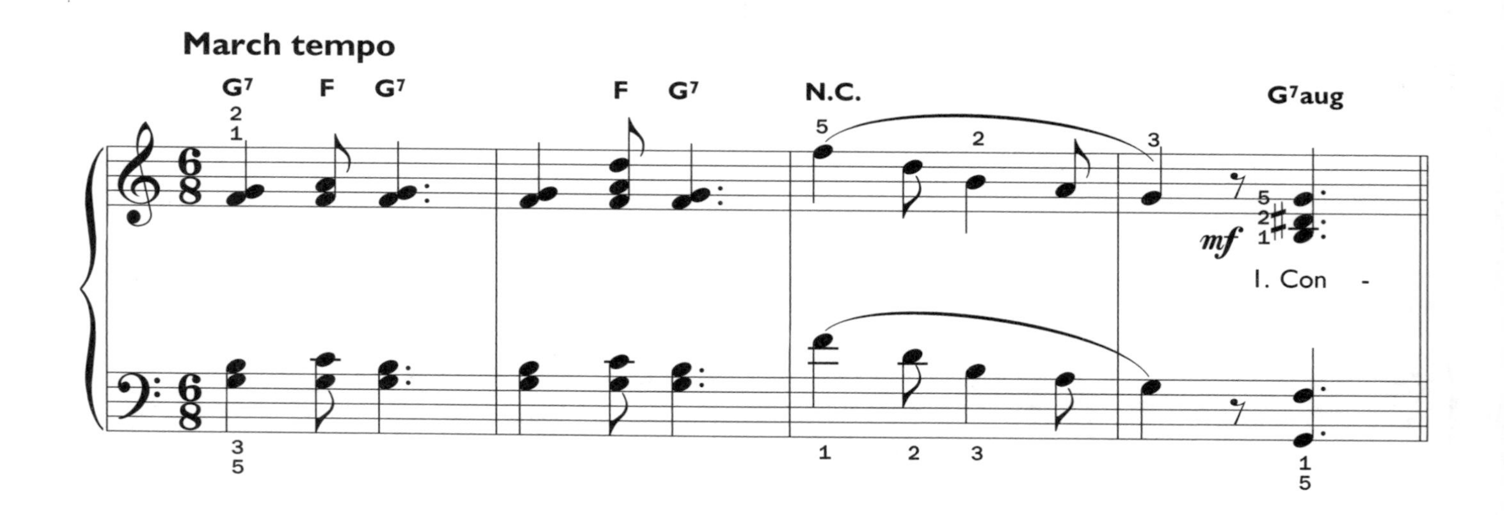

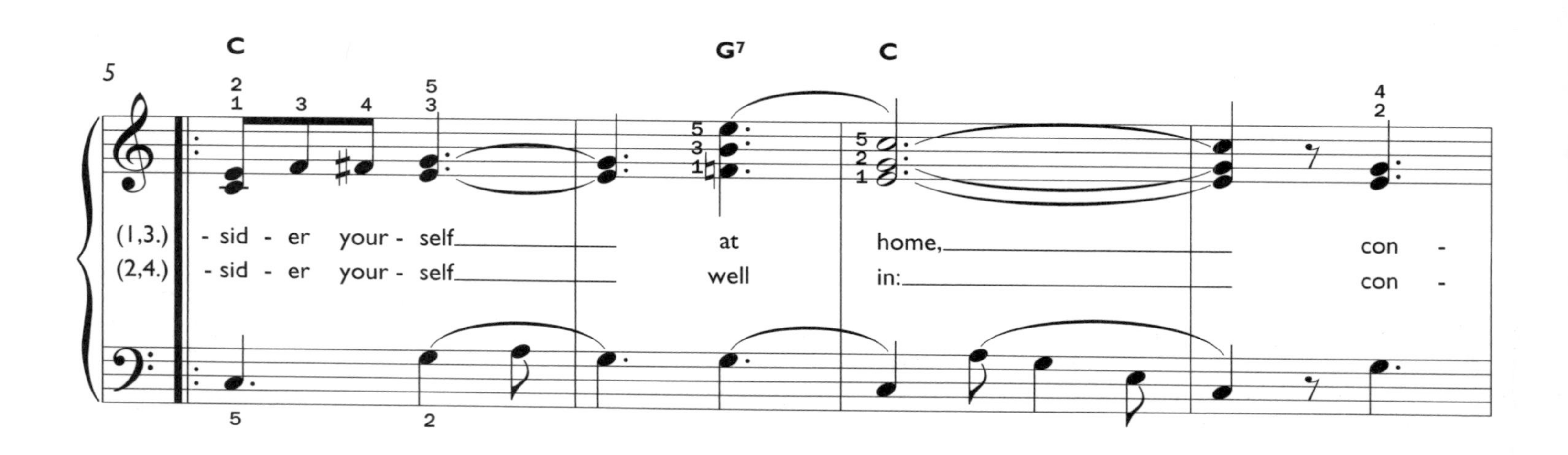

C E7 Am Gdim
tak - en to you so strong, it's
is - n't a lot to spare; who
G Ddim C D7
1, 3.
G G7aug
clear we're go - ing to get a - long! 2, 4. Con -
cares? What - ev - er we've got we
2, 4.
G Gm7 C7
share! If it should chance to be we should see some hard - days,
No - bo - dy tries to be lah - di - dah and up - pit - y,
F C7aug F
emp - ty lard - er days, why grouse?
there's a cup of tea for all.

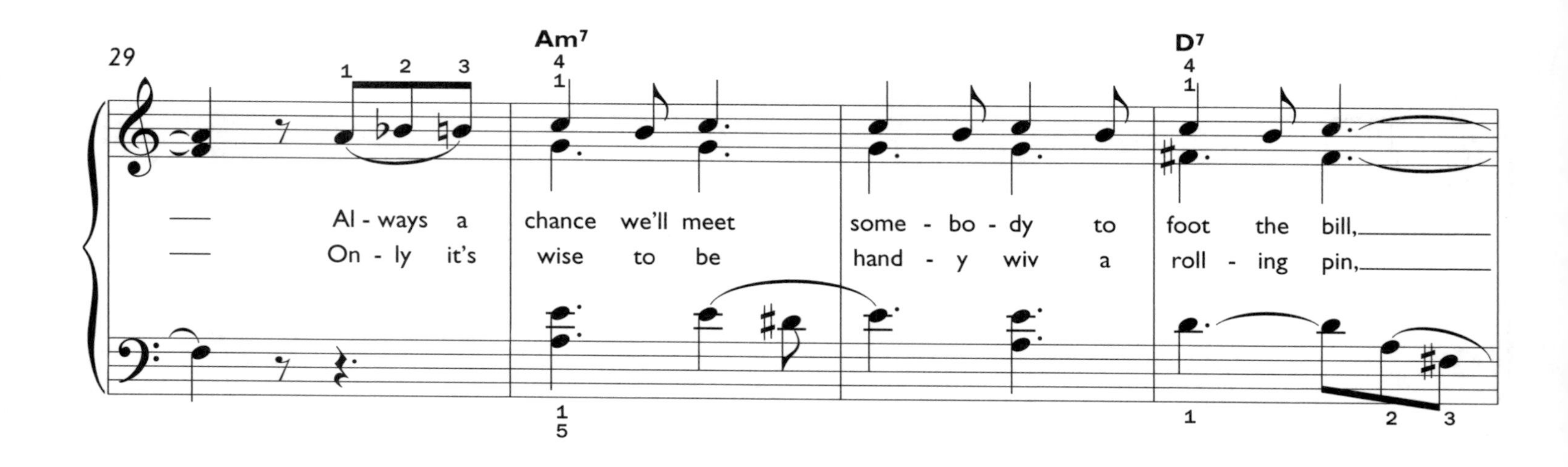
29
Am7
D7
Al - ways a chance we'll meet some - bo - dy to foot the bill,
On - ly it's wise to be hand - y wiv a roll - ing pin,

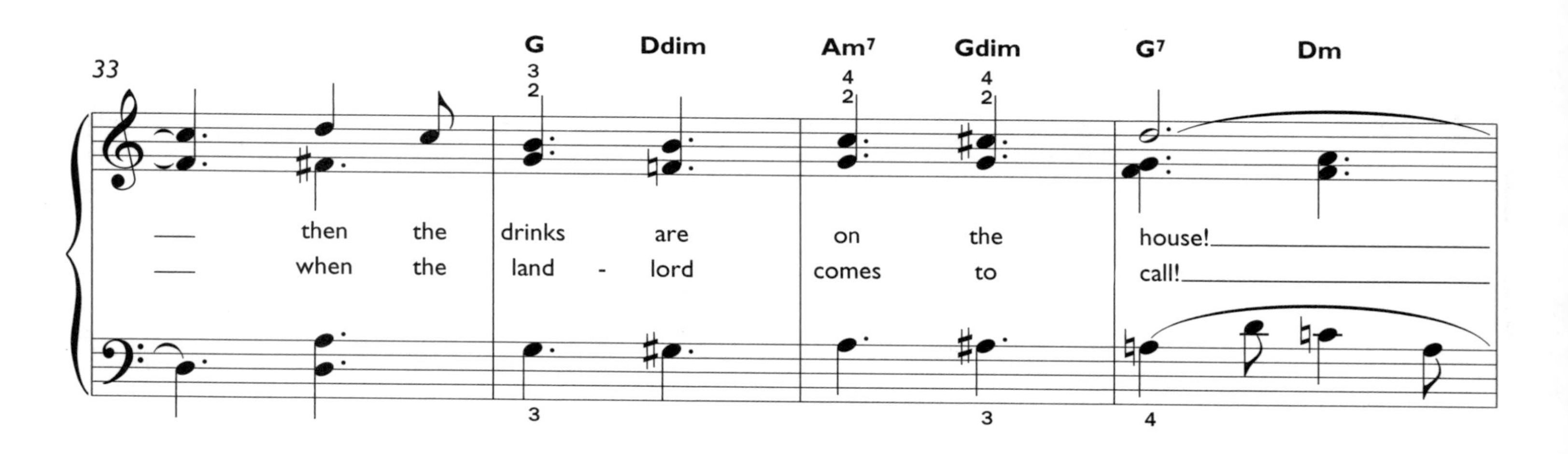
33
G
Ddim
Am7
Gdim
G7
Dm
then the drinks are on the house!
when the land - lord comes to call!

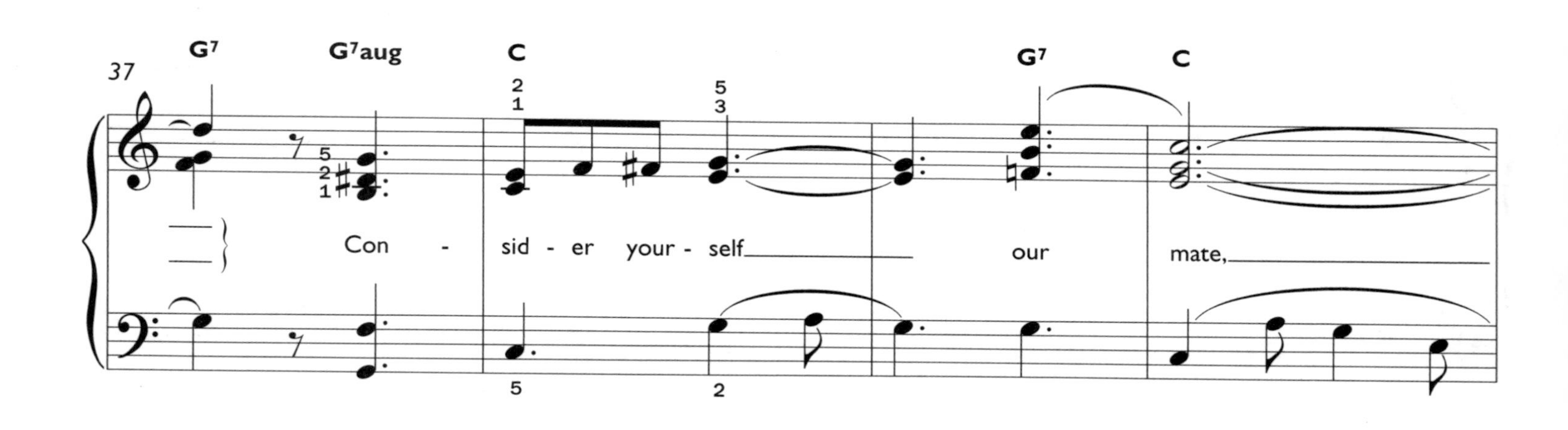
37
G7
G7aug
C
G7
C
Con - sid - er your - self our mate,

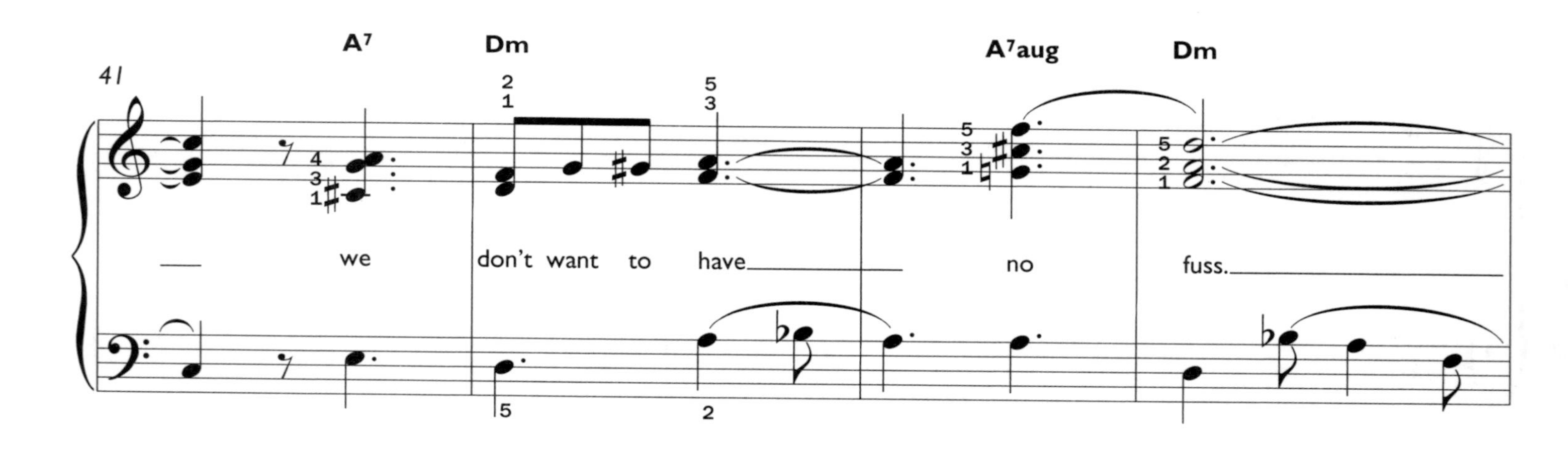
41
A7
Dm
A7aug
Dm
we don't want to have no fuss.

45
B
C
Gm6
For aft - er some con - sid - er - a - tion, we can
49
I.
A7
Dm
G7
C
state: Con - sid - er your - self one of us.

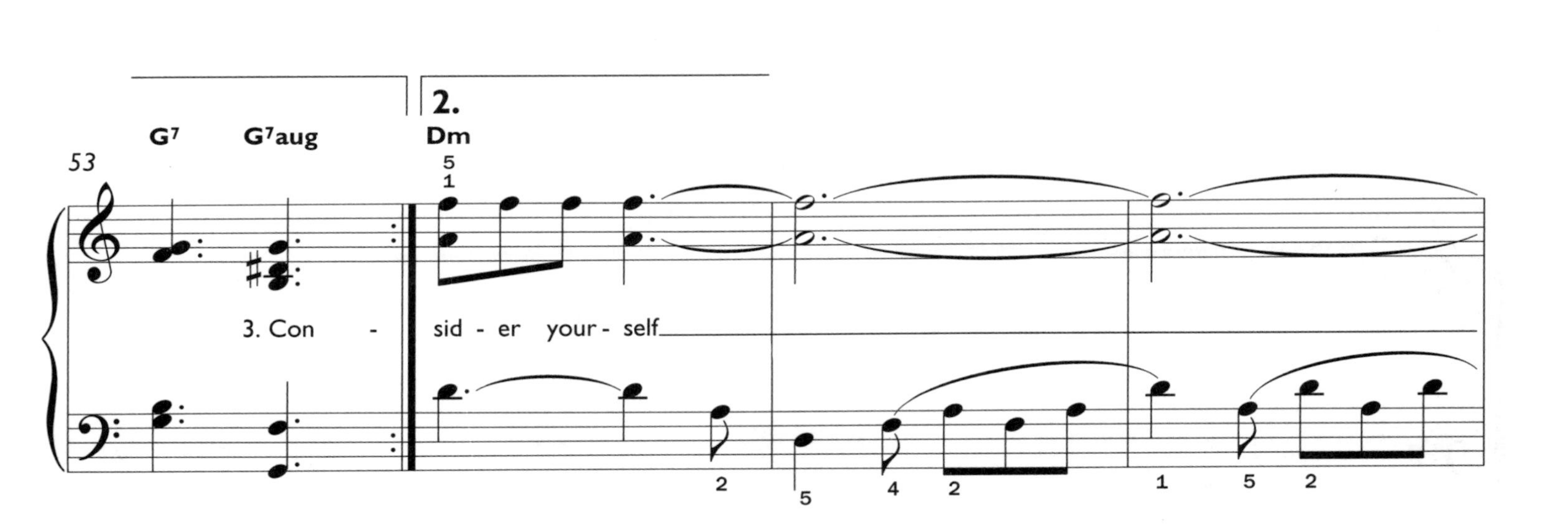
53
G7
G7aug
2.
Dm
3. Con - sid - er your - self

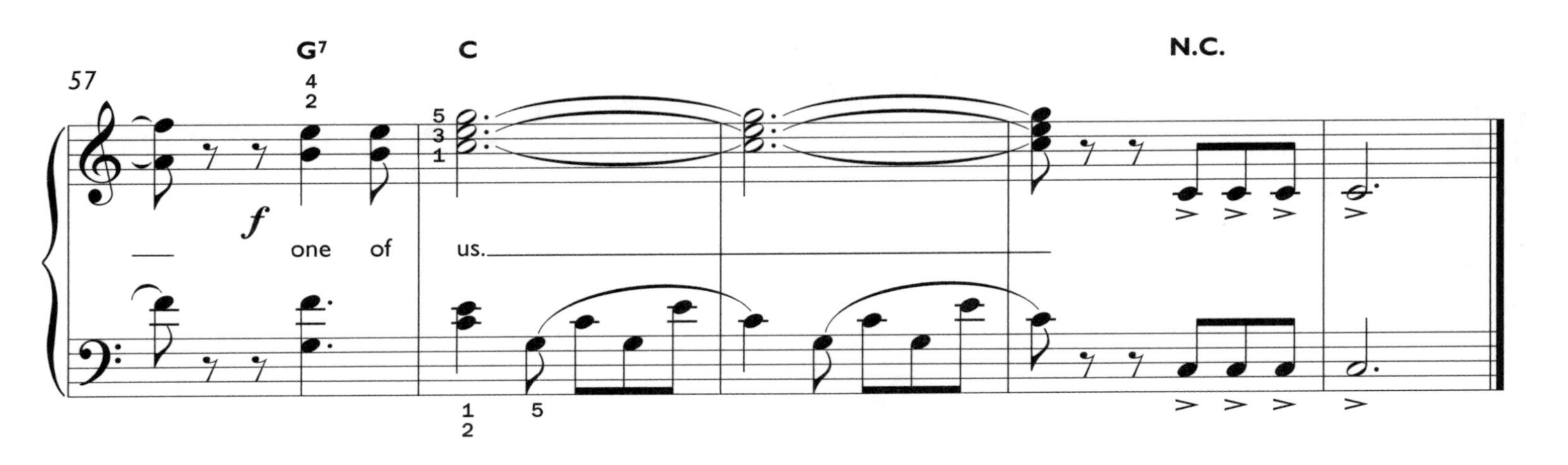
57
G7
C
N.C.
f
one of us.

Springtime For Hitler

(from 'The Producers')

Words & Music by Mel Brooks

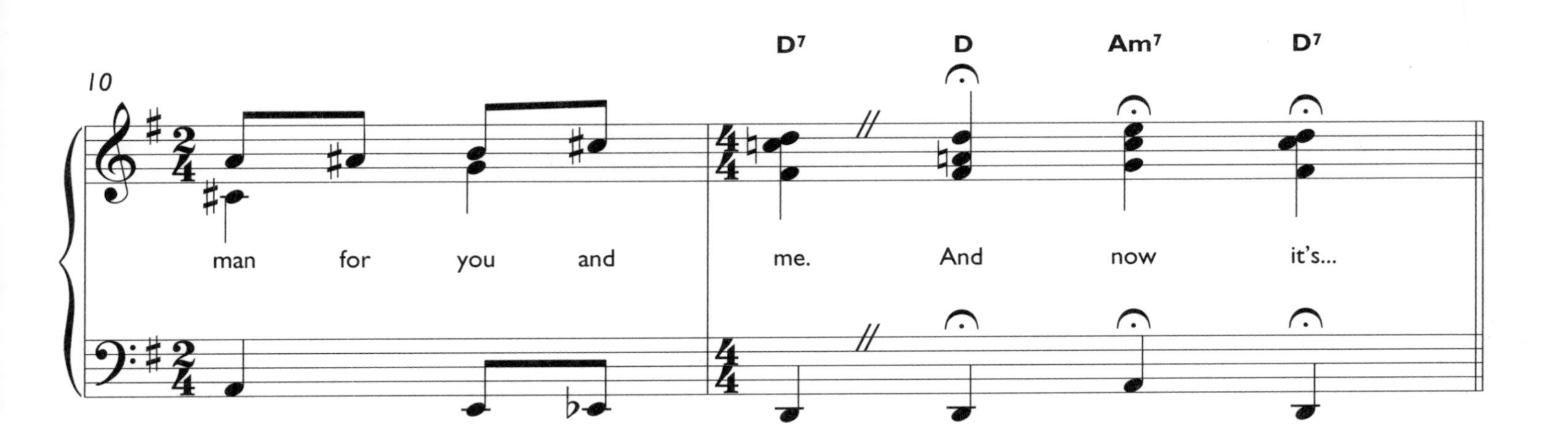
10
D7 D Am7 D7
man for you and me. And now it's...

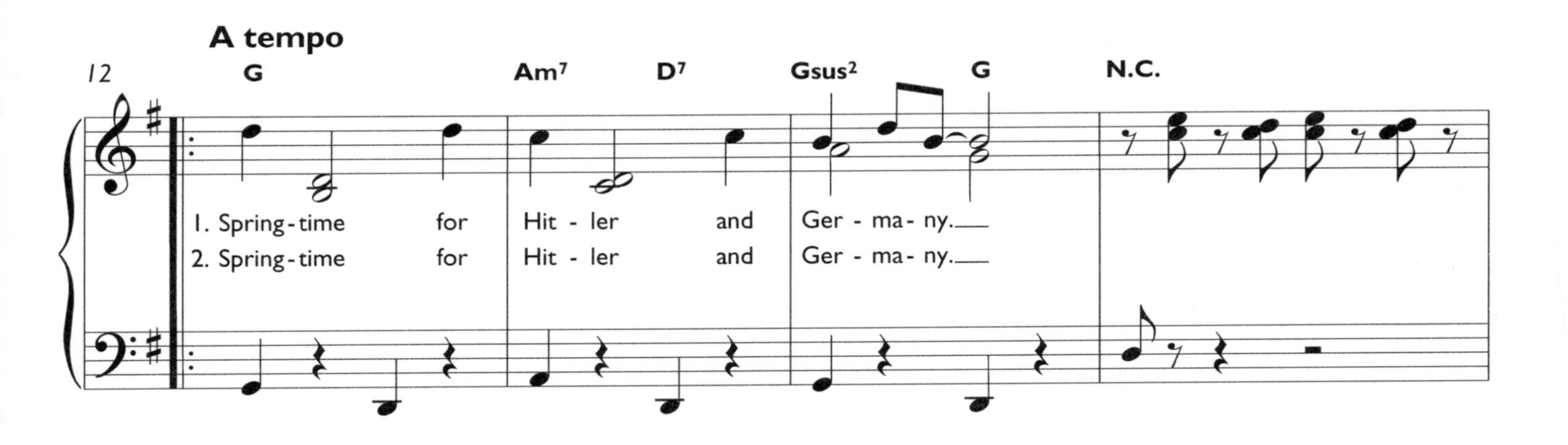
A tempo
12
G Am7 D7 Gsus2 G N.C.
1. Spring-time for Hit - ler and Ger - ma - ny.
2. Spring-time for Hit - ler and Ger - ma - ny.

16
G Am7 D7 Gsus2 G G7
Deutsch - land is hap - py and gay.
Goose - step's the new step to - day.

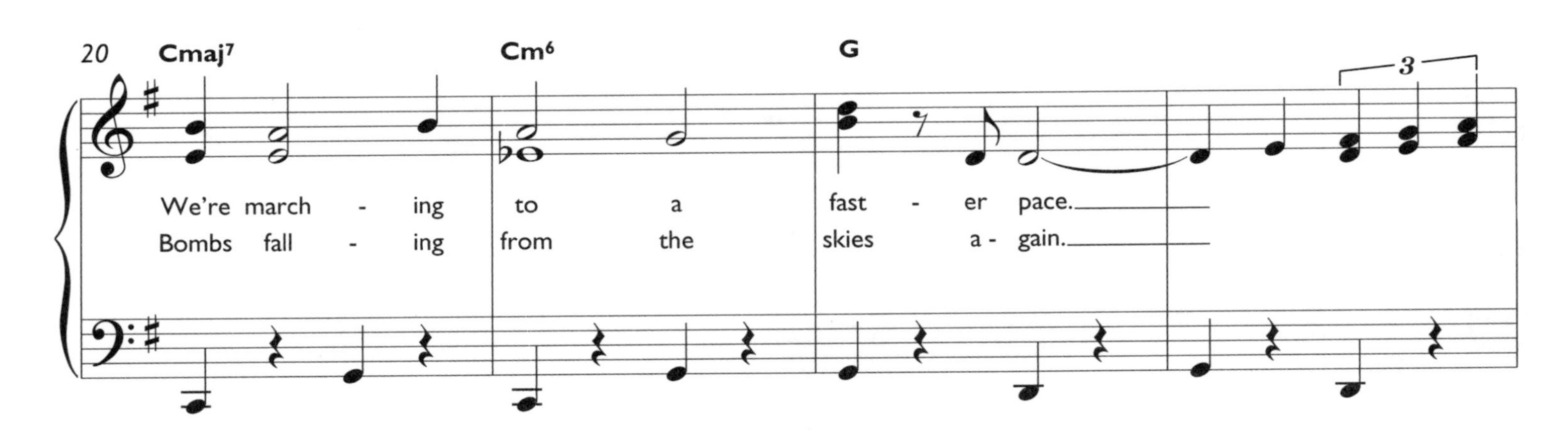
20
Cmaj7 Cm6 G
3
We're march - ing to a fast - er pace.
Bombs fall - ing from the skies a - gain.

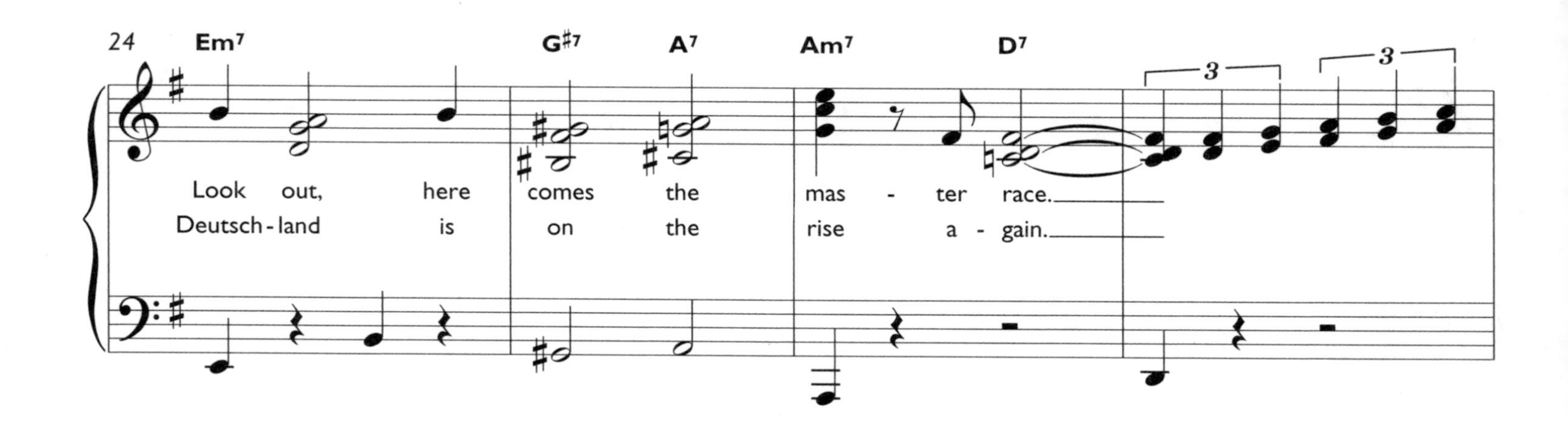
24
Em7
G♯7
A7
Am7
D7
3
3
Look out, here comes the mas - ter race.
Deutsch - land is on the rise a - gain.

28
G
Am7
D7
Gsus2
G
N.C.
Spring - time for Hit - ler and Ger - ma - ny.
Spring - time for Hit - ler and Ger - ma - ny.

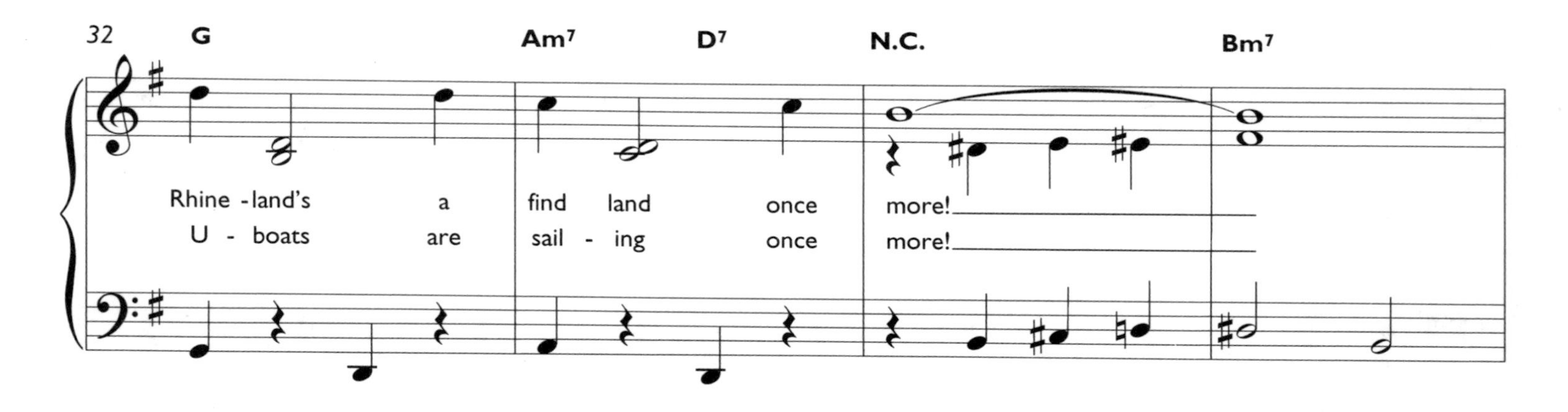
32
G
Am7
D7
N.C.
Bm7
Rhine - land's a find land once more!
U - boats are sail - ing once more!

36
Em
G/D
C♯m7♭5
1.
Cm
N.C.
Spring - time for Hit - ler and Ger - ma - ny.
Spring - time for Hit - ler and Ger - ma - ny.
Watch out

40
G Am7 D7 G Am7 D7
3 3
Eu - rope, we're go - ing on four!

2.
44
Cm N.C Am7 D7 Bm7
Means that soon we'll be go - ing, we've got to be

48
E7 Am7 D7 Bm7
go - ing, you know we'll be go - ing, you bet we'll be

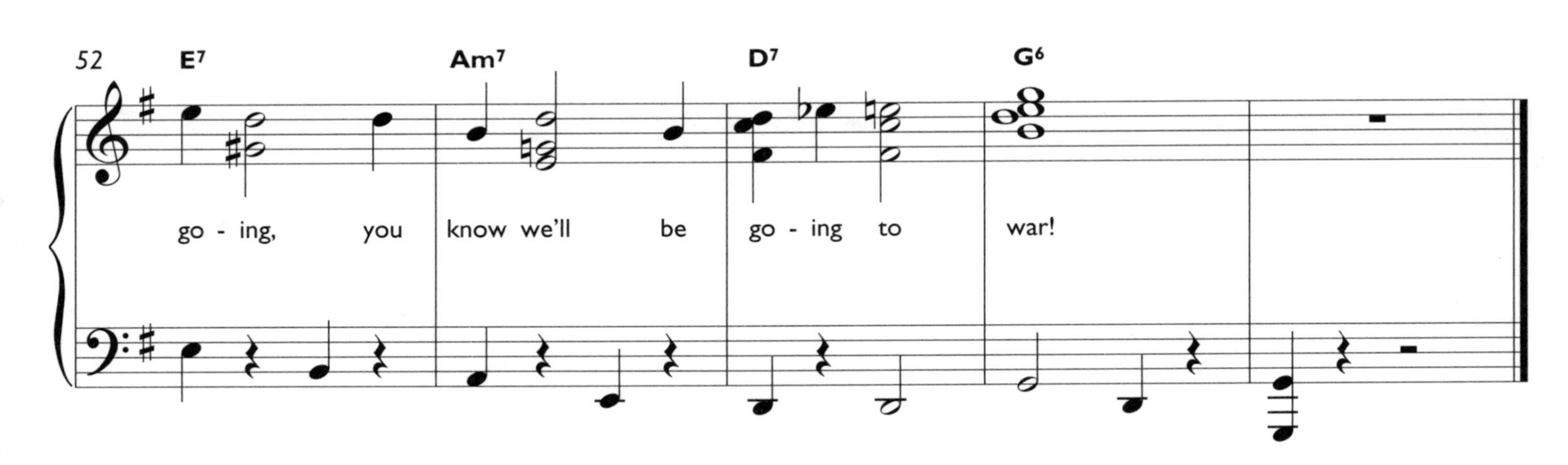
52
E7 Am7 D7 G6
go - ing, you know we'll be go - ing to war!

If I Were A Rich Man
(from 'Fiddler On The Roof')

Words by Sheldon Harnick
Music by Jerry Bock

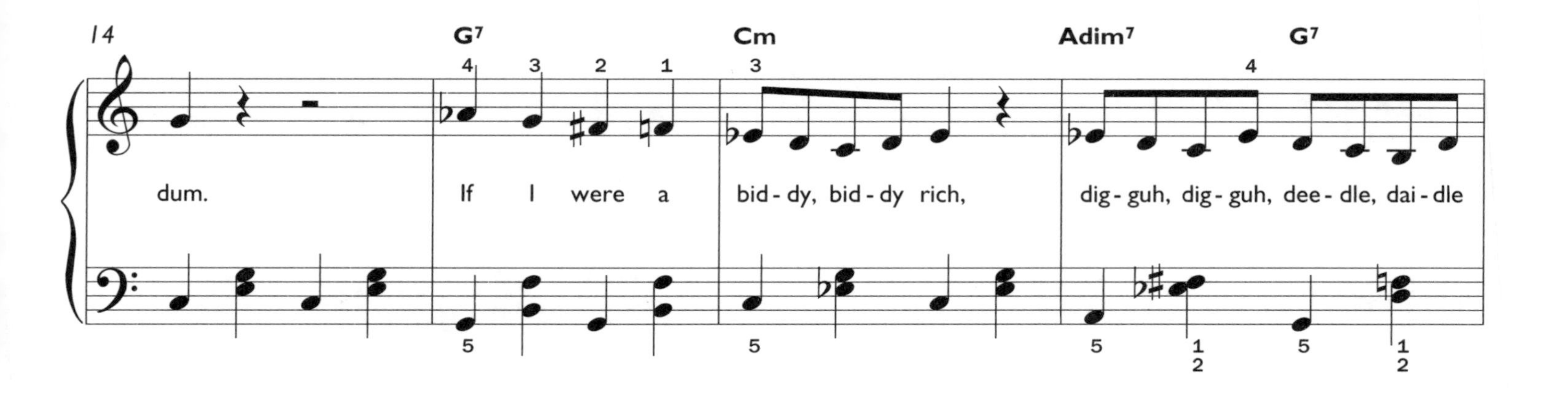
14
G7
Cm
Adim7
G7
dum.
If I were a
bid - dy, bid - dy rich,
dig - guh, dig - guh, dee - dle, dai - dle

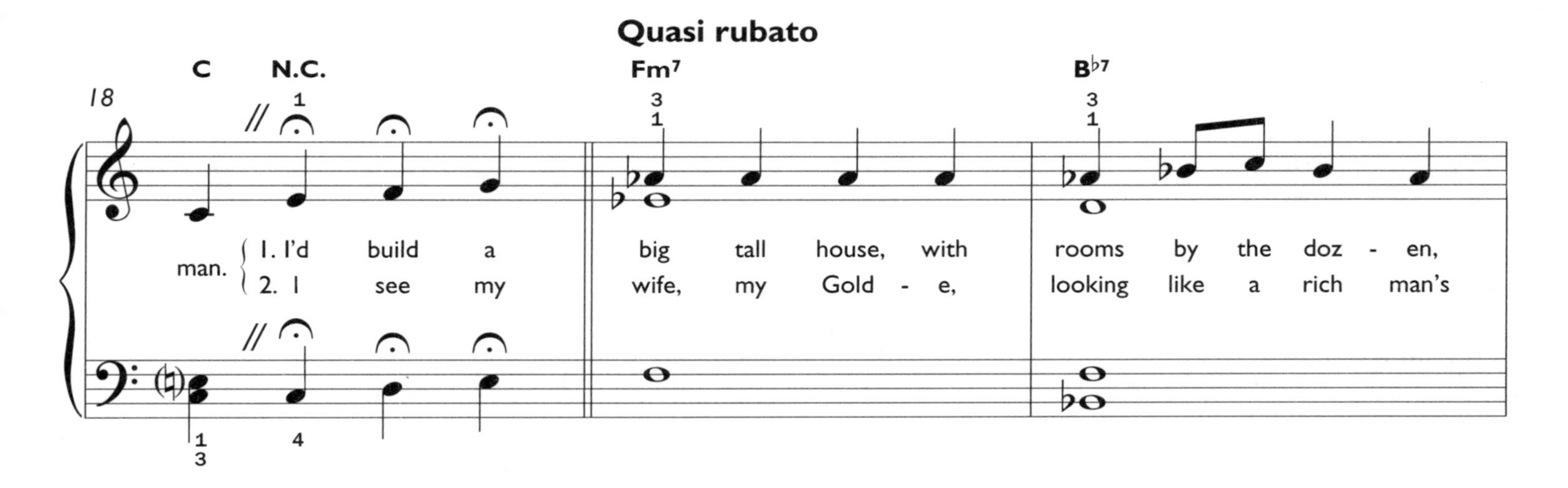
Quasi rubato
18
C
N.C.
Fm7
B♭7
man.
1. I'd build a
big tall house, with
rooms by the doz - en,
2. I see my
wife, my Gold - e,
looking like a rich man's

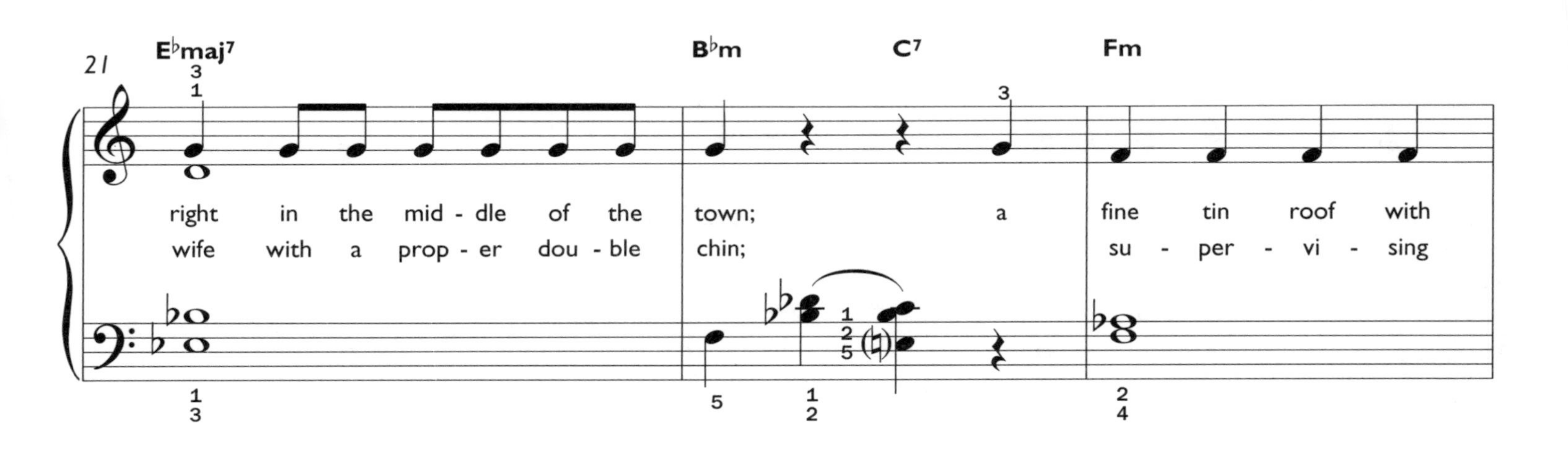
21
E♭maj7
B♭m
C7
Fm
right in the mid - dle of the
town; a
fine tin roof with
wife with a prop - er dou - ble
chin;
su - per - vi - sing

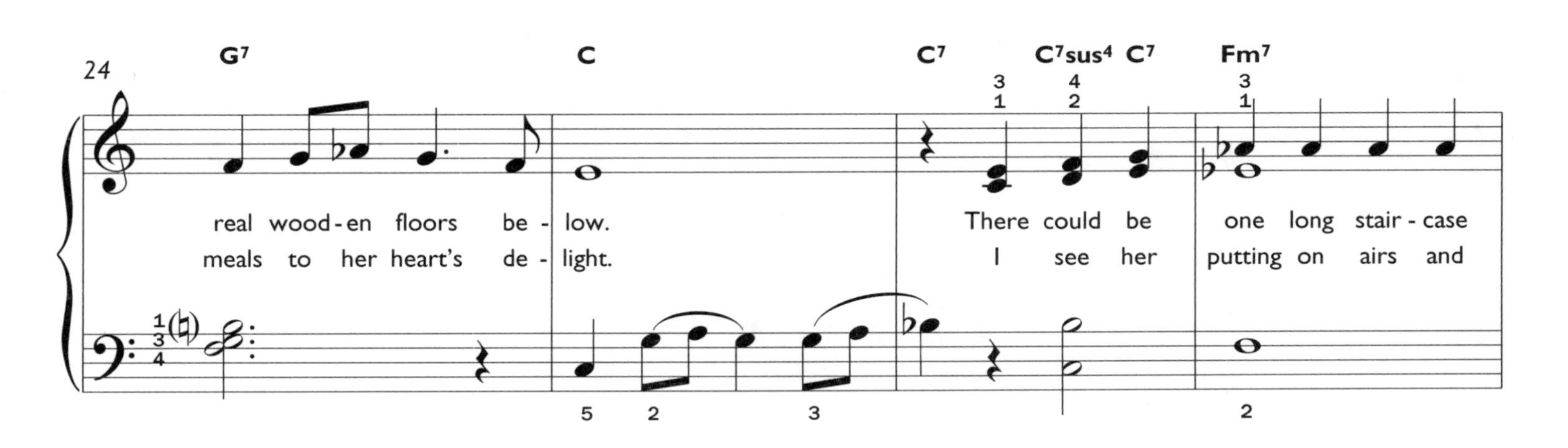
24
G7
C
C7
C7sus4
C7
Fm7
real wood - en floors be - low.
There could be
one long stair - case
meals to her heart's de - light.
I see her
putting on airs and

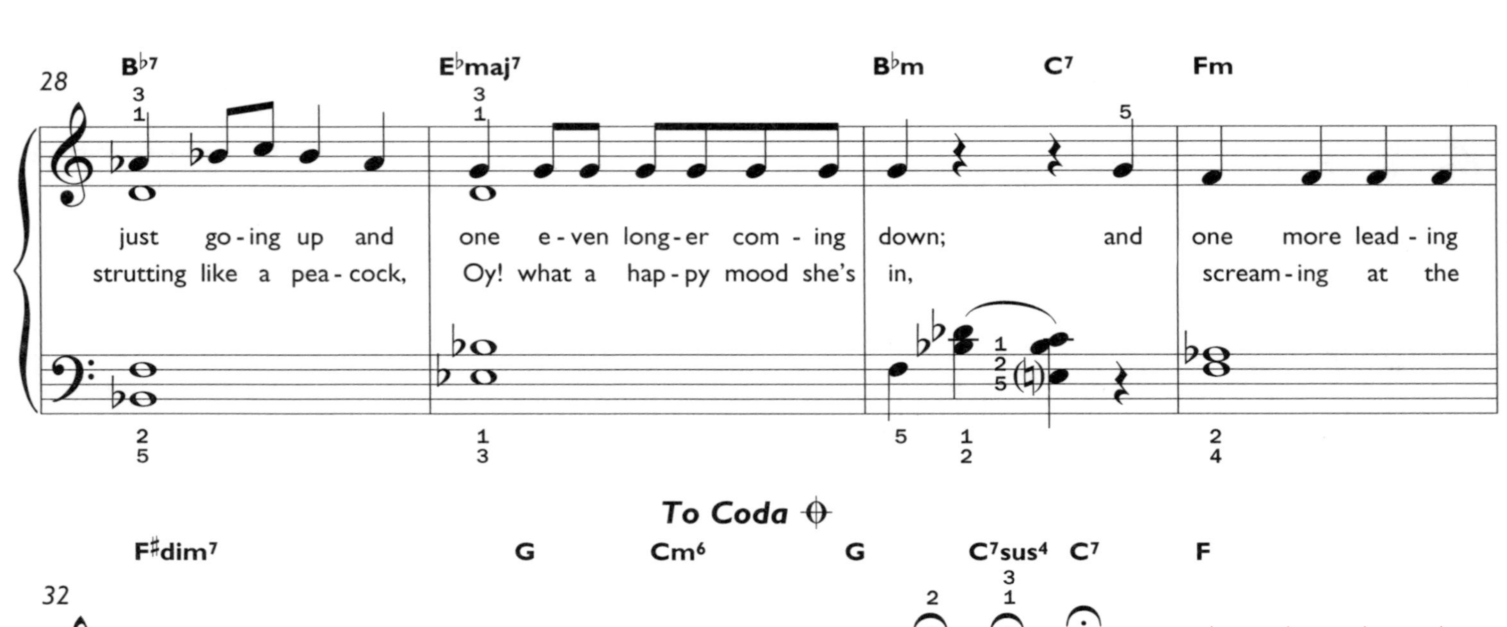
28
B♭7 E♭maj7 B♭m C7 Fm
just go-ing up and one e-ven long-er com-ing down; and one more lead-ing
strutting like a pea-cock, Oy! what a hap-py mood she's in, scream-ing at the

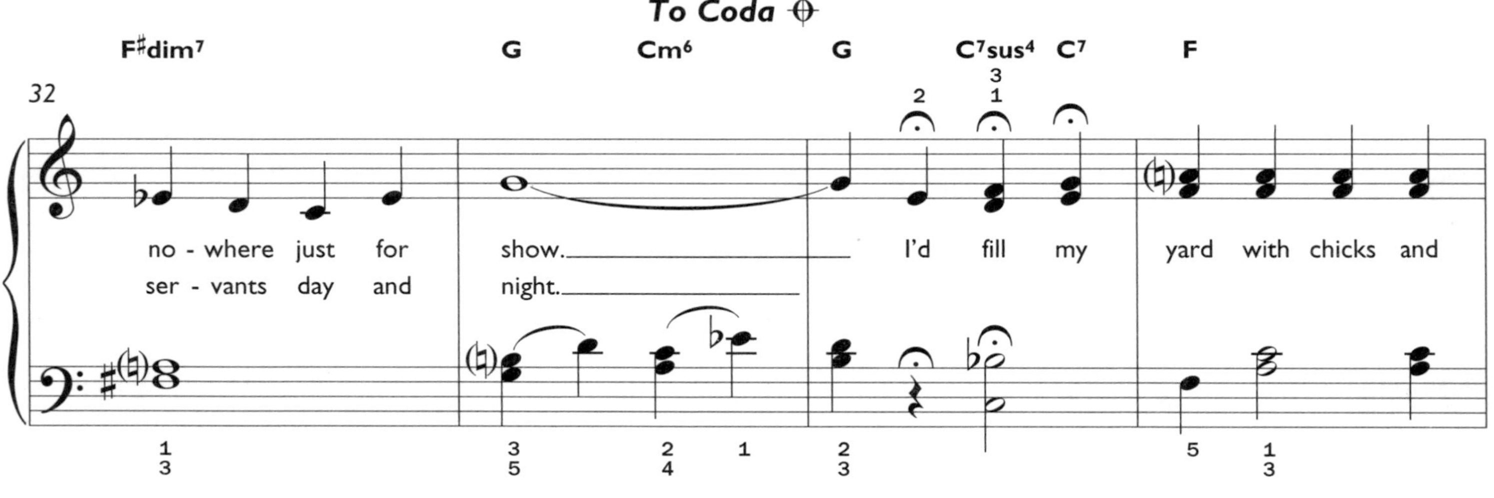
To Coda ⊕
32
F♯dim7 G Cm6 G C7sus4 C7 F
no-where just for show. I'd fill my yard with chicks and
ser-vants day and night.

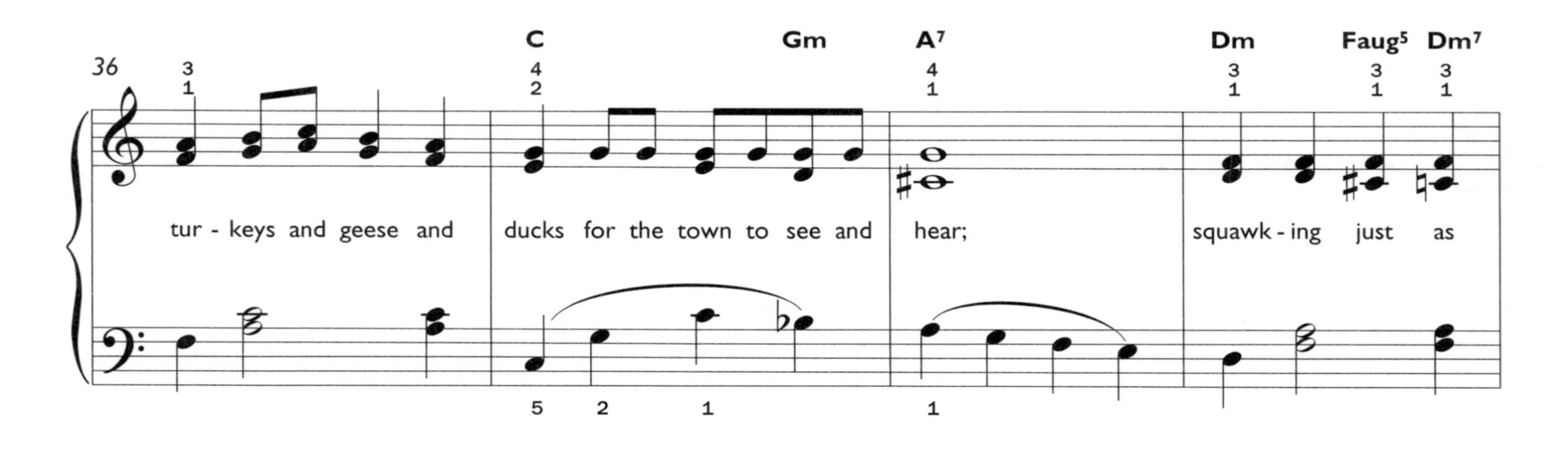
36
C Gm A7 Dm Faug5 Dm7
tur-keys and geese and ducks for the town to see and hear; squawk-ing just as

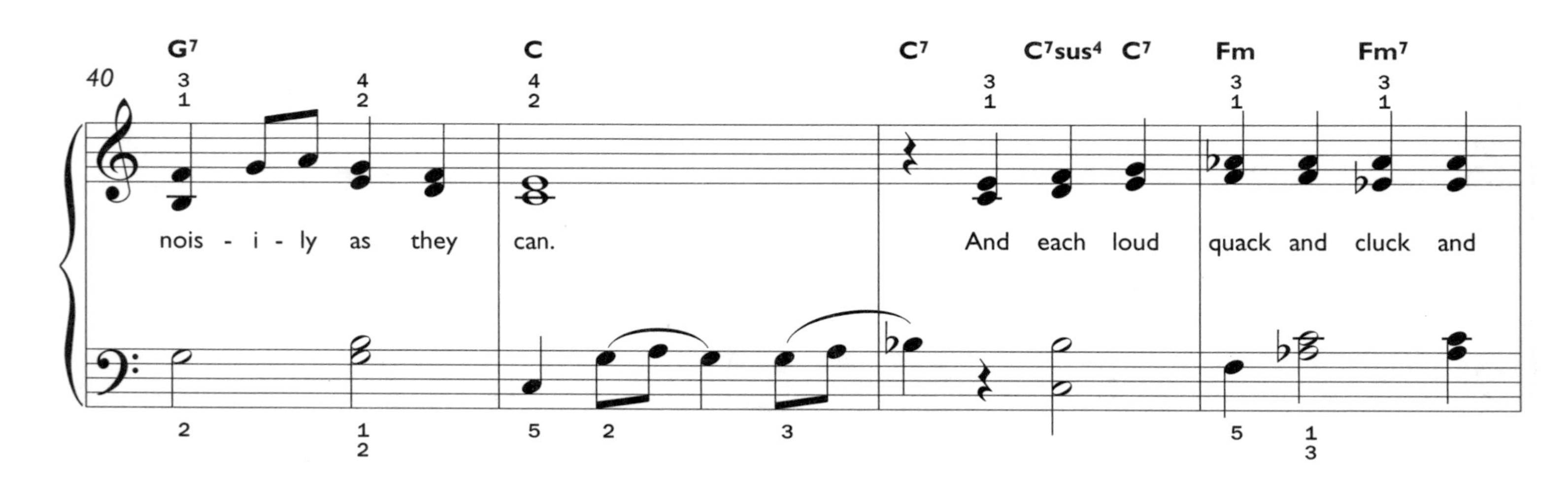
40
G7 C C7 C7sus4 C7 Fm Fm7
nois-i-ly as they can. And each loud quack and cluck and

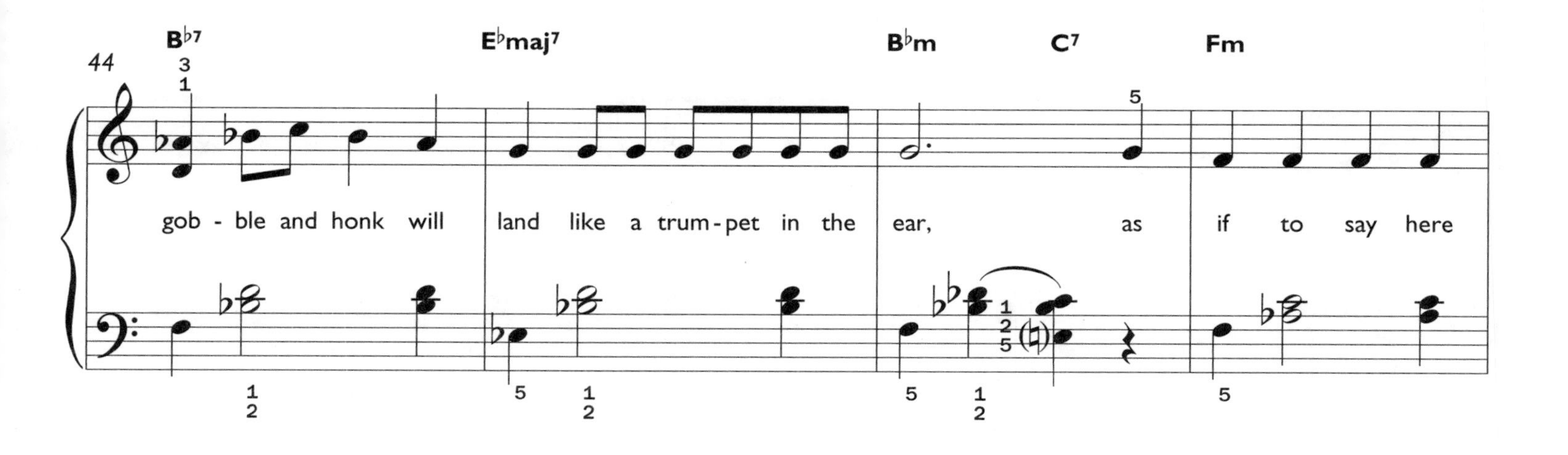
44
B♭7
E♭maj7
B♭m
C7
Fm
gob - ble and honk will land like a trum-pet in the ear, as if to say here

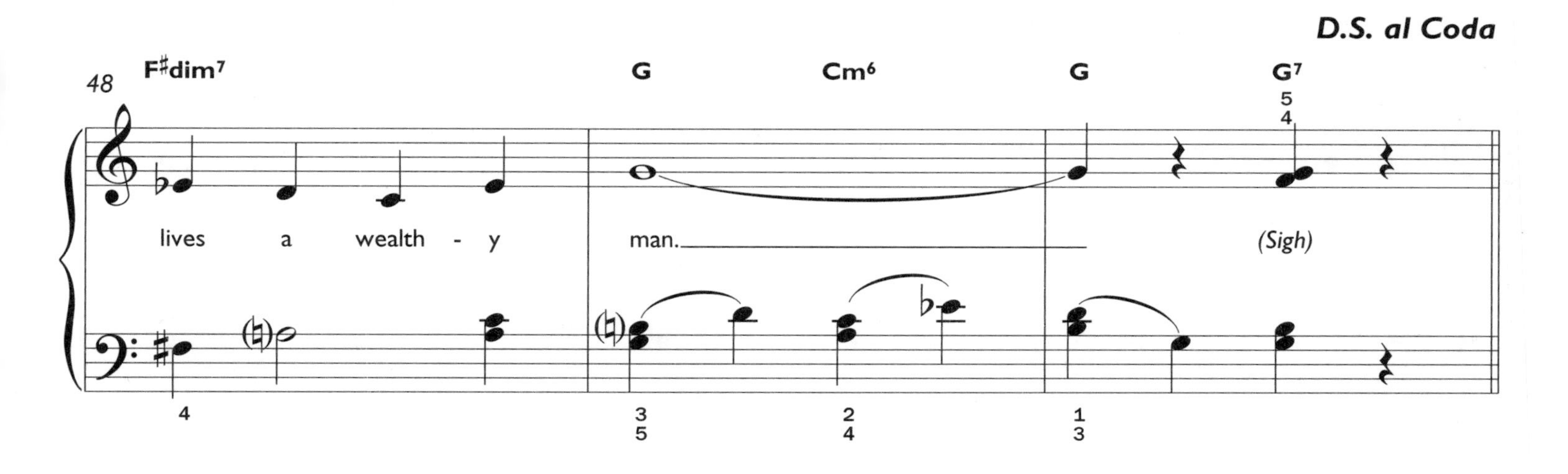
D.S. al Coda
48
F♯dim7
G
Cm6
G
G7
lives a wealth - y man.
(Sigh)

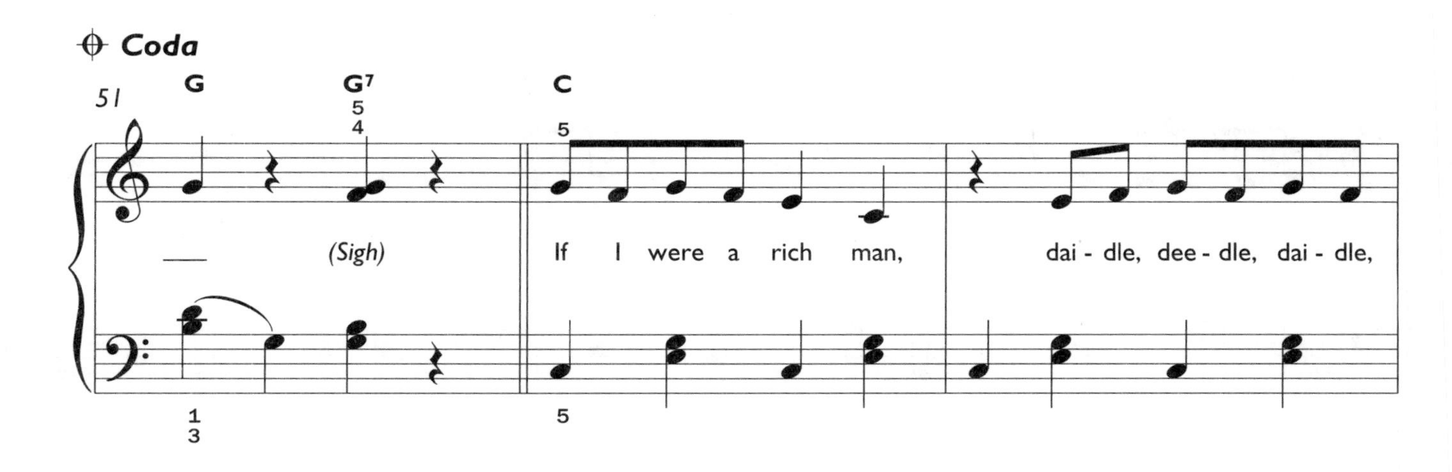
Coda
51
G
G7
C
(Sigh)
If I were a rich man, dai - dle, dee - dle, dai - dle,

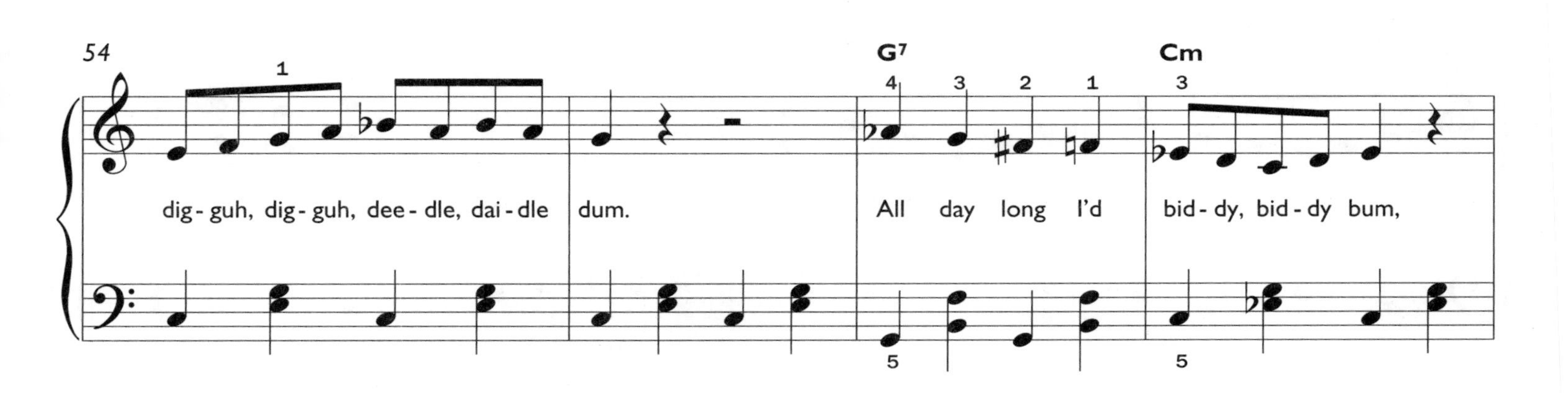
54
G7
Cm
dig - guh, dig - guh, dee - dle, dai - dle dum. All day long I'd bid - dy, bid - dy bum,

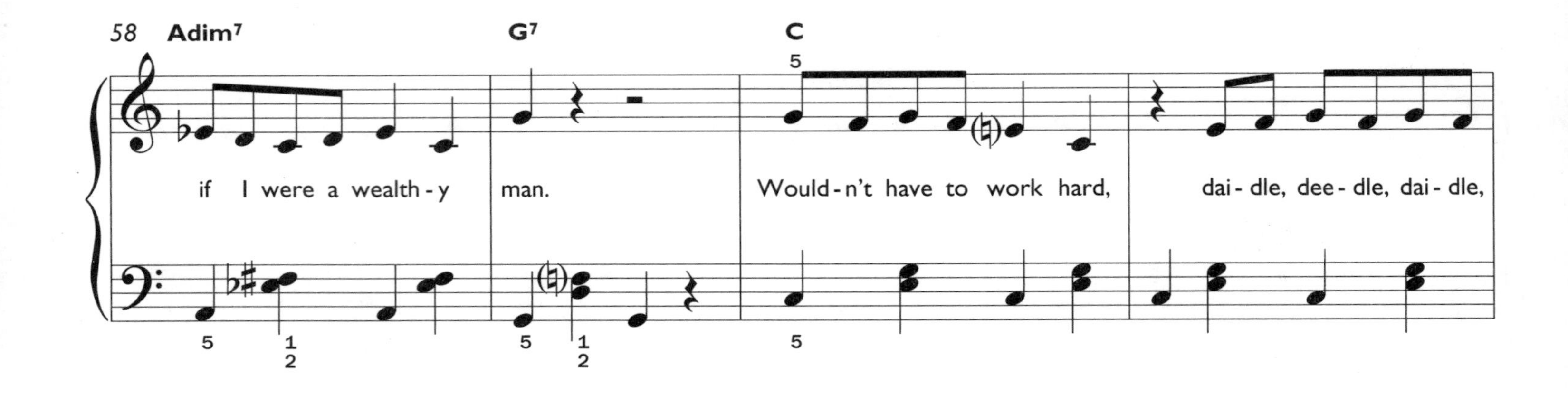
58
Adim7
G7
C
if I were a wealth-y man.
Would-n't have to work hard, dai-dle, dee-dle, dai-dle,

62
Rubato
G7
dig-guh, dig-guh, dee-dle, dai-dle dum.
Lord, who made the

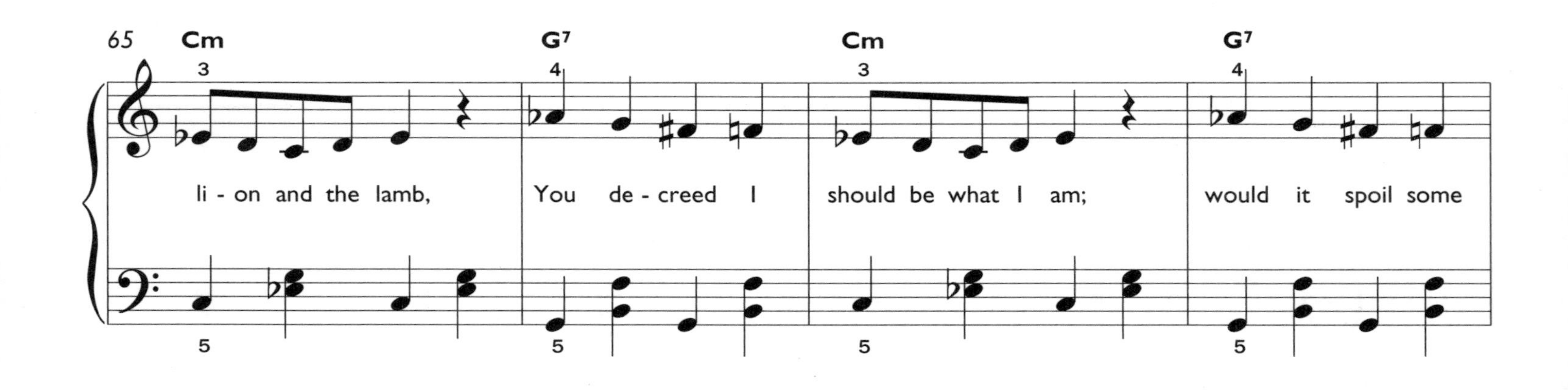
65
Cm
G7
Cm
G7
li-on and the lamb, You de-creed I should be what I am;
would it spoil some

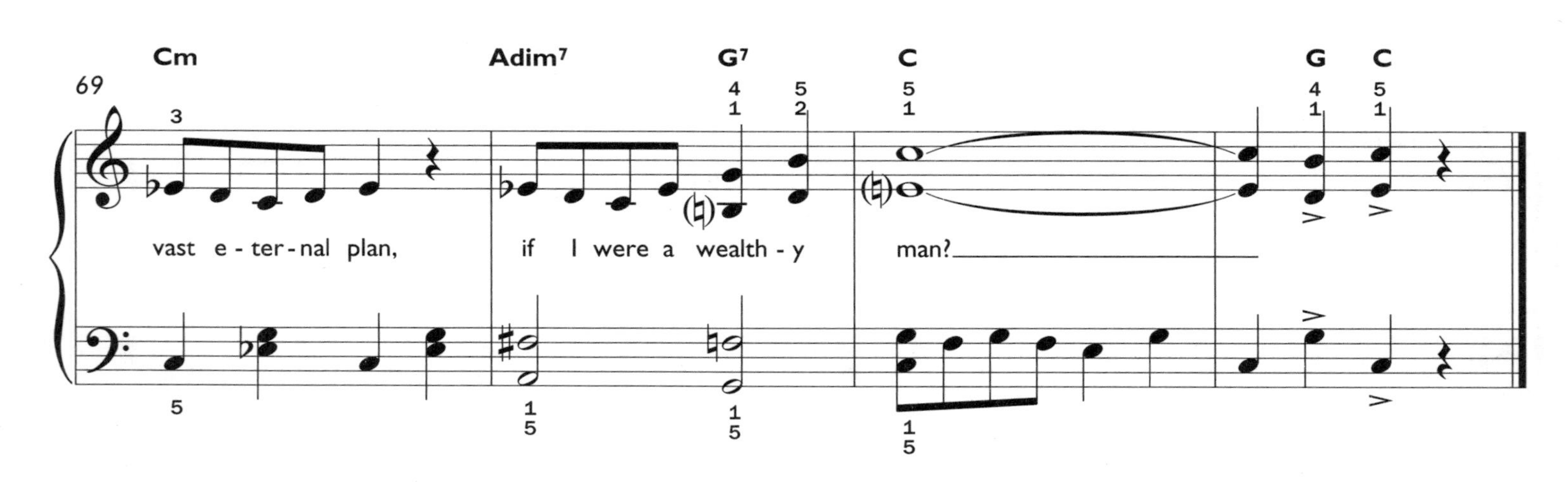
69
Cm
Adim7
G7
C
G
C
vast e-ter-nal plan, if I were a wealth-y man?

1 2 3 4 5 6 7 8 9